MW01264792

Good As Grape Juice

"Growing Better —Not Bitter— Through Adversity"

By YoYo Collins and Sandi Collins

Daylight Publishers • Broken Arrow, Oklahoma

Published in Broken Arrow, Oklahoma, by Daylight
Publishers, 2005. www.daylightpublishers.com.

Library of Congress Control Number: 2005921542

ISBN 978-0-9764103-2-4

Original 10 digit ISBN number: 0-9764103-2-X

Before my accident, I had great plans to have a career in athletics. On May 14, 1977, that changed. I could be depressed, blame God, and become bitter. That was not an option for me. I believe that what lies behind you, what lies ahead of you, and what circumstances surround you are not nearly as important as what lies within you. In spite of what the world throws at you, even a broken neck, it does not mean defeat if you really believe and apply God's principles to your life.

***You can grow better, not bitter,
through adversity.***

-Yo Yo Collins
Salina, Oklahoma
February 28, 2005

CHAPTER ONE

"Hey, Yo, that water is pretty shallow there."

"Okay," I yelled back.

The previous week-end, my friend Mike and I had scouted out and chosen a site on the Illinois River east of Tahlequah in eastern Oklahoma for a camping trip for his art club. On Friday, May 13, 1977, I had met them there after I got off work. After we set up camp we had a grand jam session before going to sleep.

When I awoke on Saturday morning, May 14, 1977, the sun was shining bright, although it was still pretty chilly for so late in the spring. Shivering in the morning coolness, I decided the bedding I had brought for the weekend camping/float trip wasn't going to do the trick another night in the 45 degree weather. Since some friends were getting married the next week, I had to cut out long enough to drive to Locust Grove for the Phelan rehearsal. Afterwards, I swung by Mom and Dad's and got my sister's sleeping bag. After visiting with them for a short while, I headed back to the river.

Around 2:30, Mike and I left the campsite and went up the river 6 or 8 miles to the 60 foot steel bridge at Eagle Bluff where I did some show-off, hot shot diving. When we returned to the campsite, we did a little fishing, whipped up a supper cooked over the open camp fire, finished the meal, had a couple of beers, cleaned up a little around the campsite, and grabbed our instruments, determined to do some serious jammin'.

Around 5:30, I felt kind of warm so I decided to dive into the river and cool off. I knew the water was shallow so I planned to barely skim the top of the water in a shallow dive, then get out, dry off, and join the others for some more music. I climbed out into a small elm tree that was hanging over the river. In spite of the shallow water, I was fully confident that I could make the dive. I went out of the tree.

My head and shoulders felt cool. I relaxed in that refreshment for a moment. Then I tried to swim to the top of the water. I couldn't move—anything!

I tried again, harder, more frantically. It was like I was in a dream—a desperate unreal dream!

I thought, "If somebody doesn't get to me pretty quick, I'm going to drown."

I concentrated on the breath that I had taken before the dive. What could I do to make it last as long as possible? How was I arranged in the water? What would I need to do if my body rolled enough that my face met the air? These questions flashed through my mind in seconds. Then I heard the sound of splashing water as some of the guys moved quickly toward me. Two of them lifted me out of the water and carried me to their van.

Mike said, "Just take it easy, Yo, you're gonna be all right."

As they laid me down in the van, I heard their conversation.

"That's a pretty bad cut - wrap it up in my shirt." They wrapped the shirt over the top of my head.

Mike said, "Yo, tell me if you can feel this."

I waited a moment and said, "No."

He repeated himself several times, but I felt nothing until he stroked my shoulder. As a physical education major, I knew that the situation was serious.

It was a short four or five mile drive to the brand new hospital in Tahlequah where X-rays were taken. After the preliminary examination, which revealed that my neck was broken, the staff determined that my injury needed more equipment and expertise than was available in Tahlequah.

Mike had called my parents and they had come to the hospital. Mom rode in the ambulance with me to Saint Francis Hospital in Tulsa and Dad followed in their car.

My head hurt badly. My right arm felt like it was stretched up over my head.

"Put my arm down, Mom," I said, but she assured me it was down by my side. I didn't believe it because my arm was hurting so much. She finally convinced me.

About an hour later, I was rolled into the emergency room at Saint Francis. The doctor at Tahlequah had said there would be a neurologist waiting for us when we got to Saint Francis in Tulsa, but it was around 11:00 before he arrived. I just lay in a side room until that time. When he finally got to the hospital, they laid me on an examination table and began to clean up the top of my head. When I had hit the bottom of the river with the top of my head, I had ripped open my scalp about seven or eight inches and had broken my neck. They scrubbed the wound, shaved the hair from all around it, and sewed my scalp back together.

Although I moaned and groaned the medical staff ignored me as they worked, talking together about trivial things, which had nothing to do with my condition, seemingly unconcerned about the pain they were inflicting upon me. I couldn't do anything about it because I was absolutely helpless, totally at anyone and everyone's mercy.

I was lifted from the examination table and laid on a Stryker Frame, a cot-looking device that resembled a stretcher more than anything else. The Stryker stood on a couple of poles and had a pivot point at each end.

Next, they used a caliper device to measure across the top of my head from ear to ear, from the back of my head to my forehead, and the circumference from forehead back around to the forehead again.

Then they brought in Crutchfield Tongs, which resembled the old ice tongs with the claw on the side for gripping the ice. Only they were not hinged like the ice tongs, but were fixed like a horseshoe and had screws through the sides on the ends.

They positioned the Crutchfield Tongs across the top of my head and just over my ears and began screwing the screws through my scalp, into my skull, so that the screws were gripping the bone tissue of my skull.

The intense pain of those screws going through my scalp and the pressure they were exerting on my skull made me think they might crush it, or at least crack it.

Again, the workers seemed indifferent about the pain they were inflicting upon me. They gave me absolutely no warning about what to expect.

They just put 'er in place, and started crankin' 'er down!

By this time, I had all I could take. With great difficulty in speaking because of decreased breathing ability from the paralysis, and with as much pure hatred as I could summon from my soul, I cried out at them, "My God, what in the hell are you trying to do to me?"

When that was finished, they pushed a tube, which was probably about the size of a pencil (but felt more like a five-eighths inch garden hose) up my nose, all the way through my nasal passage to the back of my tongue, slightly down my throat, and taped it securely at my nostril. This permitted the stomach gasses to escape more freely.

About two hours later, they brought in another stretcher that had a hole in the fabric about as big around as my face, positioned so that I could breathe when they turned me face down.

As I lay face-up, they laid the stretcher on top of my body, strapped the two stretchers together with me between them, and then rotated my body face down using the pivot points at the ends.

The Stryker allowed the attendant to change body positions easily, and with great control, to help prevent pressure sores.

When they turned me on my face, the whole weight of my head rested on my two cheekbones and my chin, and the pain from that was so much that I cried a few times for someone to turn me.

The workers took me to the Intensive Care Unit and left me with my thoughts.

I sure messed up this time. That was sure stupid of me to be so careless in that dive. Oh, how I wish I could go back and do it differently. Someone will need to call my boss at school to let him know I can't work for a while. Did they bring my car from the campsite? I'm in good physical shape so I'll probably be out of commission only about eight or ten weeks. How much is this going to cost? How am I going to pay for it?

I thought about not being able to feel Mike touching me. I remembered his statement about the cut on the head. I recalled the tremendous pain in my shoulder as if my arm was wrenched over my head when it was really at my side. I wondered why they withheld information about the sutures and tongs. At every juncture, I thought, "It can't get any worse than this!"

It was severe enough! Lying on my rotating cot I was not totally restricted to looking at the ceiling. I got to see the floor, too! I couldn't move anything except my neck and shoulders. I could only barely breathe and talk. No, it couldn't get any worse.

But then, around midnight, Dr. Shaddock, the neurologist, came into my room with my parents and told them to step over near me so that I could hear.

He said, "Your son has a fracture of the fifth cervical vertebrae, dislocation at the fifth and sixth vertebrae, and a completely severed spinal cord at that point. He will be doing little more, if any, than he's doing right now, for the rest of his life."

I was stunned and disbelieving. "Well, there goes coaching," I said aloud, but I thought, "If I have no other choice but to lie down and be fed the rest of my life, I don't want to go on."

It wasn't a thought of suicide. I'm too big a coward. And I would never have asked anyone else to take my life because I wouldn't want to place such a burden on anyone's mind and life for the rest of their life.

I was thinking it would be more convenient for everyone around me and certainly less spiritually and emotionally tragic for me if I could die some time soon.

This was long before I began to consider the Almighty, All-caring, Omniscient Will of God as an option.

Thank you, Lord, for your grace and understanding for all of us, in every situation.

I was looking forward to a career in athletics when this picture with my brother, Bennie (right) was taken.

This is our Salina High School FFA Chapter's State Champion Crops Judging Team, 1972. I am the second from the right.

CHAPTER TWO

I was in a classroom storing some books in a closet. I stacked the books over my head so high that they fell over on me and broke my neck. I awoke and realized I was having another nightmare.

My scalp itched constantly, but I couldn't scratch. After about twenty days, I realized I couldn't do anything about it, so I had to learn to turn if off in my mind.

At times I grew very hot from fever and felt helpless. I knew I couldn't get anyone's attention, so I panted like a dog because I knew that's how they cooled their bodies.

Time seemed to stop, and since my situation was so spiritually and emotionally exhausting, I learned to turn time off, too. It was as though an enormous drive, (that we, as people, have when faced with adversity), kicked in. Whatever we believe we have to do to survive, that's what we do. That was my frame of mind.

I don't remember too much about the first twelve days in intensive care except they seemed like an eternity.

With what little I could feel, I was hurting a lot. I hurt from the pressure on my cheekbones from the Stryker when I was face down. I hurt from the fever from the staff infection that developed in the laceration in my scalp. I hurt from the nightmares from the morphine. And I felt enormous regret about my stupid, careless actions in the dive that broke my neck.

Because of the fracture and dislocation of vertebrae, the surgeons took bone tissue from my hip and fused the three or four vertebrae around the injury to stabilize the vertebrae. They also wrapped some wire around the several vertebrae to assist the stabilization.

I felt very reassured, and right at home, because, coming from Mayes County you ain't fixed it in Mayes County 'til you git some bailin' warh on it!

After the surgery to fuse my spinal cord, I felt very feverish, and just wanted to rest. On Friday, fourteen days after my accident, I began to improve and they took me to a room on the fifth floor. I was still on the Stryker frame and could see nothing but the ceiling and the floor.

Immediately that Friday night, folks began to visit me. First, my mom and dad came. Then a girl I had been dating visited and, after her, some cousins dropped by.

The next day was Saturday and beginning at 8:00 a.m., a steady flow of people made their way into my room until after ten o'clock that night. Sunday was filled with as many folks as Saturday, and, because it was Memorial Day weekend, Monday was the same.

I said to my dad, "I've just got to get out of this. I've got too many beautiful people pulling for me."

I was determined to overcome the situation for myself, but, because of their support, I thought, "I must persevere. I can not let them down!"

The emotional support I experienced from family and friends continued during the first five months of hospital and rehab center care. Not a day passed that I didn't receive at least a card. "Pretty amazing," I thought.

I remember feeling so fortunate, so thankful, to have so many people who helped me maintain a good attitude and a strong emotional state of mind. People brought me special things to eat, took me to the park, and cared about me.

I have to say that this was not the case for so many of the patients in rehab who had little or no support from others. Although I was in bad shape, I knew that, in comparison to so many others, I was very fortunate. Even to this day I feel so grateful for this blessing.

The morphine I got for pain, the fever from the staff infection, and the psychological trauma of the realization of total paralysis affected my sleep.

My cousin's wife was a registered nurse. She suggested that the stroke of a hand on my neck or shoulder would reassure me, helping me to rest easier. I didn't feel like I needed this stroking, (sounds pretty macho, huh, guys?), but it amazed me how much security was in a touch. It sure felt good and was welcomed. To this day, I love something as simple as the feel of Sandi's finger lightly tapping my chest or face. (Husbands, we need to touch our wife's arm, back, neck, or face, just to be touching her. It feels great and it's great communication.)

Shortly after I was admitted into the hospital, they began to give me medication—Uroquid Acid to help create an acid base in my urinary tract, an antibiotic for the staff infection, and other pills.

I had trouble getting them down from my prone position. There was the danger of choking and, had I choked, I could have suffocated before I could get help. I dreaded having to take them.

I hadn't eaten in quite a while and one day I happened to think, "Why am I having so much trouble getting these pills down? If that was a big ol' piece of steak, I could swallow a bite almost as big as a biscuit!"

After that, when the nurse came in with the pills, I thought, "Steak! Big, juicy, delicious steak!"

After that I didn't have any trouble. Now, especially if I'm sitting up, I can swallow them by the handful.

At any rate, I thought I was progressing pretty well and that my self-assurance and determination to survive would pay off.

But I had not yet learned that it is only through God's Holy Word that we can believe correctly, and only He can give us direction and action. I did not know that His ways bring us to survival and that any other way ends ultimately in defeat and destruction.

CHAPTER THREE

"Doc, it's my *head* that's hurt, not my *stomach!*" I said one afternoon after about twenty-one days of IV's, water, and glycerin. "Get me some food in here. I'm about to starve to death!"

He took out his stethoscope and listened for some "stomach sounds," as he called them. "Okay, we'll see about getting you something in the morning."

The next morning, a nurse's aid came in and said, "Breakfast!"

"All right," I said, pleased that I was finally going to get to eat. "What is it?"

"Oatmeal."

I had anticipated that I might get steak and eggs, or at least that's what I had hoped for, but I was glad to get anything.

I was still lying flat of my back on the Stryker frame, unable to move. She brought the first very large spoonful of oatmeal down toward my face. I opened up like a baby bird and gobbled it into my mouth. I closed my eyes and just enjoyed chewing. (Have you ever taken the time to chew oatmeal? Try it some time.)

As I was leisurely chewing my delicious breakfast, I happened to look up and here came another spoonful! My mouth was already full from the first bite, but if I didn't open my mouth, she was going to pour it all over my face.

So, again, like a baby bird, I opened my mouth as wide as I could to make sure I got it all in. With two spoonfuls of oatmeal in my mouth and no time to swallow any, here came another spoonful! I imagined the headlines:

YOUNG MAN SURVIVES DIVING ACCIDENT,
DROWNS IN OATMEAL.

At that point, I determined that I was NOT going to drown in oatmeal. I reconciled myself to the fact that this lady was going to pour it all over my face. So I closed my eyes again and waited for the inevitable. A second or two passed *and no oatmeal in the face.* I peaked out of one eye to see what was going on. She was standing there with the spoonful right over my face. I quickly closed my eyes again, turned my head, and somehow made her understand that the next time I opened my mouth, I did not want it filled with oatmeal. I wanted to tell her to slow down.

Several days before they took me to the rehab center, they removed the Crutchfield tongs from my head and took me off the Stryker frame. Next they put me on a regular hospital bed. Then they fitted me with a neck brace to stabilize and provide traction to my neck.

Because of the inactivity, I was most comfortable with the temperature at about 85 degrees. However, for the comfort of the workers, the hospital temperature was between 65 and 70 degrees. On my June 20th ambulance ride to rehab, I enjoyed the 92-degree temperature.

At the rehab center, they took me to my new room and bed in the afternoon, and the rest of the evening was rather uneventful, aside from getting fed and setting up house. I was anxious for the next day and the beginning of work.

Before long in the rehab center I began to realize that they weren't going to help me get out of the wheelchair. They were beginning to train me to live in the wheelchair. Realization and depression sunk in about the same time.

The first thing they did was assign a wheelchair to me. It had a very tall back that would recline and foot/leg rests that would elevate. I had been lying down, had not been in a sitting position, for almost 40 days when they brought me to rehab. My body had become so acclimated to lying down that, for about the first four days, when they sat me up in the wheelchair, the blood would rush from my head and I would pass out if they didn't recline the chair. I had to re-learn how to sit up!

I also still could only move my head and shoulders, and neither of them very well, thanks to the neck brace I was wearing. This was not long after the bra burning by liberated women in America and the neck brace was so annoying and irritating that I swore I would have me a brace burning when they took it off for good.

It was several weeks before I began to have any return of muscular control, anywhere on my body. The gross majority of my paralysis was permanent, but some was only temporary, due to swelling and pressure associated with the injury. The first return began at my shoulders and gradually worked its way down to the control I have now. First were the deltoids, the muscles that go down over the shoulder and enable us to raise or flex our upper arm. Next were the biceps, the muscles that enable us to make a muscle or flex the lower arm. Next came the wrist rotators, flexors, and extensors. Last, over a year after my accident, I had a slight return in my triceps. Since about a year and a half after my accident I have had (at most) very little, or no return.

After I learned how to sit up again, I was taken to Occupational Therapy (O.T.) and Physical Therapy (P.T.). O.T. was my first formal rehabilitative activity and it began with my therapist placing a peg between my fingers and thumb, and asking me to put the peg in a hole in a vertical board hanging on the wall while I was sitting in my wheelchair. I had to raise my arm a little bit to get it up to a position where I could do this. I could hardly feel the peg, and I had tremendous difficulty in raising it above elbow height and extending it just a few inches to the pegboard. I had to make several stabs at the board to finally get one inserted into the board, and when the therapist handed me another peg, I thought, "What's the use in stickin' pegs in a board?"

I was very disgusted at these seemingly senseless and ridiculous menial tasks, but, like I had learned to do in so many other circumstances in my life (especially in athletics) I did what my superior said, to the very best ability I could.

Three months passed and I had enough return in my left wrist flexor muscles that the prosthetics craftsman began to fit my left hand and arm with a tenadisis (pronounced ten-uh-dee'-sis) splint, which was a device that utilized the wrist flexors into a controlled pinching action. When he was finished in a few days, I said to him with a light-hearted determination to overcome my paralysis, "What are you going to do when I come back in about eight months and throw this thing in your face?"

He looked at me sternly, without a smile, then looked back at his work as he said, "You won't bring it back."

I thought, "You don't know how determined I am."

However, the prosthetics craftsman was much closer to the truth than I was, as I still use the same tenadisis splint to this day.

Physical therapy gave me no more hope for total recovery from the wheelchair than O.T. However, they did talk about and begin to work on strengthening certain muscle groups. This was familiar and interesting to me since I had just spent two years in concentrated study of the subject.

I went to work as hard as I could. I didn't know where it was going to take me. But at this point, although the life that lay before me was very uncertain, I pretty much thought that I was in charge and that it was up to me to decide where I would go from there.

At that point I didn't know that the Lord already had great plans for my future.

CHAPTER FOUR

"How did you get through it?" People ask this familiar question often, expressing their amazement. Then they add, "I don't think I could live with it!"

Before my accident, I was oblivious to spinal cord injury. I soon found that about one spinal cord injury a week comes into the rehab center, a statistic which is heightened by the summer months of activity among predominantly very active and less inhibited young men.

The result is often permanent paralysis. These people are termed either paraplegic, or quadriplegic. Para means 2 limbs. Quadri means 4 limbs. Plegia means paralysis. Paraplegia is either partial or total paralysis in 2 limbs, usually the legs. Quadriplegia is either partial or total paralysis in 4 limbs. If a paralyzed person has total control of his/her fingers, hands, and arms, he/she would be paraplegic. I can move my arms and wrists, but I can't grip with my fingers, so I am quadriplegic. The amount of care needed is far greater for quadriplegics because of their inability to grip with their hands.

I saw several in the rehab center who were totally crushed by similar accidents and circumstances. They seemed to be unable to recover a positive sense of direction for their lives. I was affected severely. It was an utterly devastating experience. But the answer to the question, "How did you get through it?" is very simple. I got through it by the grace of God. I got through it by the training He had given me before my accident and by the support of the people He has placed in my life. And I live with it by that same grace from God! We never know what we can do, or what He can do for us, until we are faced with the situation. I have to admit, at times it was very inconvenient for me!

I have a skin condition called seborrhea, which makes itchy, scaly spots on my head and face. Mine is a mild case, so I was able to control it with normal grooming before my paralysis. After my accident while on the Stryker frame, with the staff-infected cut on my scalp, grooming was everything but normal. Sometimes I would have to lie there and itch for hours and hours without the ability to scratch my own head. Finally, I learned to block my discomfort from my consciousness by filling my head with thoughts of other things. It was no easy task, but I was able to do it!

They had shaved my head around the laceration in my scalp to facilitate cleaning of the wound. At the time, my hair was five or six inches long and at some point I decided they could clean my head and get to my itchy spots better if my whole head was shaved!

It was a brave and rash act to order this haircut and, although it *did* accomplish the desired purpose, I really didn't like the way I looked!

Through the years I had always been glad no one took a picture of me without my full head of hair. Then, to my surprise, Sandi produced, from some hidden source, one that was taken three months after my accident.

Here I am, three months after my accident.

When the doctors told me my spinal cord was severed and I was permanently paralyzed, I thought, "That's it! My life is over!"

I knew I was going to live, but when I became aware of the fact that life as I knew it, or life as I had planned it, had definitely changed, I knew it was something I was going to have to face. I had to decide where I was going to go from there.

My six months stay in the hospital ended and I returned home to spend most of my waking hours staring at the TV and wondering about how I was going to have a useful life.

At times I was mad at myself, pretty disgusted about how stupid I had been to do what I had done.

Before the accident, I had been confident of a bright future. I had finished Northeastern Oklahoma State University in Tahlequah with a major in physical education and a minor in music. My dream was to coach baseball and/or basketball in some high school and eventually graduate to coaching at the college level.

Then on May 14, 1977, my dreams were shattered and I had little to look forward to.

Although I was confused and at a loss about where I was going to go from that point, I knew I had to do the best I could with what I had.

I had been brought up in a stable, positive family environment. Because of this, even while lying immobile, able to speak only a few words at a time, able to take only shallow breaths, and depending on morphine for pain every few hours, I knew that depression or bitterness could serve absolutely no purpose.

I didn't know then that *"All things work together for good to them that love God, to them who are the called according to his purpose"* (Romans 8:28). I didn't know that God was going to teach me how to breathe in His presence and breathe out my doubts.

Although this miracle didn't happen instantaneously, God began to work in my life, beginning with music. I knew God had given me my musical talent. Why, music was even responsible for my nickname. When I was two years old there was a song that was popular on the radio, titled, "I Love My Little YoYo." My dad saw me playing on the floor and remarked, "You're my little YoYo."

It was a nickname used, at first, only by my dad. Mom kept calling me Kenneth Wayne, and some aunts, uncles, and cousins would call me *Kenny Waynie*. But, gradually, most people began referring to me as YoYo and by the time I was ten or twelve years old, even Mom had shifted to YoYo. In time I was simply *YoYo* to everyone.

I loved athletics, and it was to athletics that I looked for my career. As an athlete, it was part of my personality not to be afraid to do whatever it took to get something done. I had so many good experiences in athletics in school, but it never came easy.

When I was very small, I longed to be able to hit a baseball well, so I began diligently to study and practice the mechanics of hitting. A lot is involved - choosing a bat, developing a correct stance, foot placement, correct stride and weight distribution, correct pivoting of the feet, hips, and shoulders, exact timing of the extension and follow-through of the arms and wrists, the position of the head and eyes, and calculating, as exact as possible, the plane of travel of the ball to align the travel of the bat to the same plane.

That's just the mechanics of hitting. (There's another aspect called the psychology of hitting!) After several years of study and practice, I came to a point where I thought I might have developed a pretty good swing, so I asked one of my coaches to come with me to the field to watch my swing.

We got out the pitching machine so he could carefully watch the execution of my swing. He put a ball or two in the machine, I got my bat, stepped into the batter's box, and the coach turned on the machine. As the machine threw the ball, I concentrated as best I knew how on my stance, head position, rhythm, timing, and execution of the best possible swing I could perform. When the swing was finished, I looked over at Coach and said, "Well, what do you think?"

He said, "That's as good a swing as I have ever seen. You only did one thing wrong, Yo."

I said, "What's that?"

"You missed the ball!"

It didn't really matter what else I did or didn't do in my swing, if I missed the ball, the rest of my efforts were in vain.

When I went to my first baseball meeting in college, I anticipated that the level of competition and ability of the players on this team would be greatly improved over what I was used to. This meeting was in the fall before spring practice began. The coach wanted to get a general idea of how many might be trying out. He gave us each a card to fill out in order to gather a little more basic information, like where we were from, what position we played, how we threw and batted, and so forth.

I had a dream of pitching, but I figured I ought to concentrate on the position I had the most skill in, in order to make this team. By the word Position on the card, I wrote "Outfield (can Pitch)." I started both years in the outfield at N.E.O. A&M Junior College, and did as well as most on the team. The only time I pitched was in a very tough situation in the last inning of a game in my second year.

Then I graduated and moved on to the four-year state college at Tahlequah. When we filled out the cards there, I thought, "I'm gonna fool them."

When I got to the word *Position*, I wrote "*Pitcher* (can play outfield)." I pitched both years at Tahlequah, but they wouldn't let me play outfield!

I always had to really work at whatever I did. Now, I was determined to walk again. I was going to show the world that I could do it! I knew I would get out of that wheelchair!

But after a six-month stint in the rehabilitation center, I left the hospital in my wheelchair. I was still determined to beat the wheelchair, but it just wasn't happening.

Something else had begun to happen while I was in the rehabilitation center. I had begun again to sing a little, but I had no idea how God was going to use the talent He had given me to give direction and purpose to my life.

I pitched for my college baseball team at Northeastern State University.

CHAPTER FIVE

I drank alcohol when I was in high school and quite a bit when I was in college. I always wanted to drink responsibly and sort of prided myself in having discipline. But, I must admit, several times I really got plastered and looking back, I wasn't doing a very good job at controlling my drinking habit.

Because Thursdays class schedules in college were usually light, parties and beer busts were always on Wednesday nights so that we could sleep it off the next day. One Wednesday some of the guys were going to Kansas to party. In Oklahoma the legal age to buy beer was 21, but in Kansas it was 18.

That night I just had to say, "No," because I had some tests that I had to study for. About five of the guys came into my room about a dozen times, and said, "Aw, come on, Yo!" I persisted in explaining that I could not go and that they would have a great time without me. They finally left. I thought they had gotten the message, so I returned to my studies.

About ten minutes later, some eight or ten of them came into my room, grabbed me, picked me up, and carried me out the door. I began kicking, biting, scratching, and cussing, in an effort to get them to put me down so that I could stay in my room and study.

But they had ganged up on me and I was no match for them. They took me out to Dave Bowman's little Ford Falcon, shoved me into the back seat on my stomach, and four of them sat down on me. We rode to Commerce just up the road about five miles toward Kansas, and stopped at a liquor store to get some booze. When they stopped, Dave said, "Go ahead and let him up, guys. I think we're too far for him to do anything now."

But I had to get back. So, as soon as they let me up I got out of the car and bolted back down the road toward campus. A couple of them came after me for a short distance, but soon they let me go. I settled into a hearty jog and began to watch over my shoulder to see if they were coming after me. I had gotten several football fields away by the time three or four of them bought booze and came back to the car.

It was after dark. I was running on the side of a very busy highway. The lights from the traffic were keeping the road illuminated pretty well. When the car began to pull out of the liquor store, it started coming my way. I picked up my pace until the next car passed me. When the road was dark again, I ran off the side of the road and lay down in a ditch of tall grass.

I thought I was far enough away. I didn't think it was light enough for them to be able to see where I had gone off the road. But they came up just past where I was lying, made a U-turn in the road, and stopped on the shoulder very close to where I was.

Whoever was on the passenger side rolled his window down and said, "Come on, Yo, if you're that determined to go back to campus, we'll take you."

I thought, "Well, that's the least they can do, after putting me out like this."

I got up and went back to the car. When I got in and closed the door, Dave pulled away from the shoulder onto the highway. When he had attained about 35 miles an hour he said, "SUCKER!" We were on our way to Kansas.

Another time I was so drunk when we came in from partying, that they stood me up against the wall to get a mattress out from under me, and I never knew it. I was not that drunk very often, probably six or eight times in a three-year span. I never would have made an alcoholic because every time I got drunk, I was sick as a dog for the next three days. It didn't take me long, a couple of years, to figure out that I didn't ever want to get drunk. The thrill just wasn't worth the price of the pain afterwards.

By the time I was in school at Tahlequah, I had practically quit getting drunk, and, in fact, was not drinking much at all any time.

"It has come my mature time," I thought, "to only drink socially and to enhance a good time."

That was the way it was the day I broke my neck. I had drunk only two beers with supper that evening. I certainly wasn't drunk. I was a grown man, 23 years old. I could handle this dive with just two beers without any problem. I had done it many, many times. I was in control of this thing. I had it under control.

At that time, I absolutely denied that alcohol had anything to do with my accident. I was proud to be a man in control of his life. But I'm convinced now that those couple of beers was just enough to cause me to be over-confident in a very comfortable, yet dangerous, situation. I believe, now, that if I hadn't had that beer, I would have waded out to cool off instead of diving.

But like so many others, I simply tried to out-smart, out-do, and out-think the devil, foolishly thinking that I could deal with him on my own.

But I didn't have the ability to see (spiritually) that the things that I was doing (physically, that were against the laws and principles of God) were going to end in tragedy. I was living in a way that was leading me further away from God—a way that ultimately ended in loss and destruction.

God didn't cause the accident. I caused the accident by doing something I knew was dangerous. Therefore, it was reasonable that at first I was just mad at myself and blamed myself for the carelessness that put me where I was. I also knew that it was very possible that the two beers I had that day impaired my judgment, and my ability to dive, more than I realized or would admit at the time.

I got through blaming myself and decided to buckle down and prove the doctors and therapists wrong. I wanted to show that I could recover and walk again.

My athletic accomplishments had always been the result of much effort. I wasn't afraid of hard work and believed that if I just worked at it hard enough, I would reach my ultimate goal.

But I did not walk again. Eventually, with surgery and physical therapy, I regained the use of my arms and wrists, but I had little feeling in my hands, with no motor control in my fingers.

My life had always been consumed by physical activity. When I wasn't playing baseball, I was hunting or fishing. Now I was paralyzed from the collarbone down.

Church wasn't a part of my life. I had become a Christian when I was 9, but I quit attending church by age 15 or so. I figured I could get along without church like Dad and a lot of other people around the community. My attitude toward God was borderline atheistic at this point, but God was so loving and patient in bringing me His Word and His people.

I began to study God's Word, the Bible, with the same type of persistence and determination I had once employed in athletics.

I had believed that the *religious stuff* was for the old and the weak, but as I studied I began to realize that it was true! In comparison to the power of God and the power of Satanic or demonic forces, all of mankind falls in the weak category.

While lying immobile on that cot which allowed me to be manually turned by two people from my back to my stomach, I was able to take only shallow breaths. When I spoke, it was to utter only a few words. Depending on morphine every few hours to kill the pain and knowing that all that was happening to me in the hospital was simply preparing me to live forever in a wheel chair, I said, "That isn't my goal. My goal is to get out of this chair!"

However, a year and a half passed and I was still relying on my chair, but God was at work, reshaping my attitude and my purpose in life. What had been a great tragedy in my life was about to become a blessing.

Although my father was not saved until Sandi and I had been in the ministry for eight or ten years, he applied a lot of good Christian principles in his life, such as honesty, loyalty, integrity, hard work, and being a good neighbor. My mother was a Christian and took me to church. When I was nine years old, I declared my faith in Jesus before the members of Salina First Baptist Church.

By the time of my accident, I had abandoned my church and its teaching, but, in spite of this, God had not abandoned me. He was always there, trying to bring me to Him, even though I continued to resist. I am thankful that God had patience with me until I got His message!

Coming to this realization didn't happen right away, I am sorry to say. When I got home from the hospital on December 9, 1977 I had begun to work through my problems on my own. I decided that I had to have a change in attitude.

Just a couple of months after the accident I began to remember some sound principles I had learned in athletics -the principles of persistence, determination, perseverance, self-discipline, self sacrifice, and goal setting. I began to put them to work in my present situation. I began to realize that what was behind me and what was ahead of me and what circumstances surround me was not nearly as important as what was within me.

My first goal was to move something - anything. I was always trying to move my fingers, my toes, my legs, or my arms.

I was lying in my bed one day in the rehab center. I had already finished with physical therapy. My roommate had gone for his therapy session, so I was alone in the room. I had been working on trying to move anything and everything. I had begun to feel some nerve impulses going down my left arm to the biceps muscle. That's the muscle that pulls the forearm to the shoulder, the bend-your-arm muscle. I had been working specifically on this movement for several days.

This day, the impulses were getting stronger and stronger, so I kept pulling harder and harder, and the impulses kept getting stronger and stronger, and I kept pulling harder and harder and harder...and I finally pulled my arm up! But then I couldn't get it down. I had to wait for someone to come in and put my arm down, so I could bend it again. Great, I had reached my first goal.

Along with the goal to move something, I wanted to sit up in a wheelchair and use my prosthesis to hold several tools and utensils to feed myself.

After my stint in the rehabilitation center, I went back to Salina still determined to beat the wheelchair. I offered to teach some classes in anatomy at the high school in exchange for physical education students helping me with my physical therapy.

I realized that consciously I had rejected God, but subconsciously, I was obeying God's principles of self-discipline. I have found that the truths and principles, which apply to our lives, are available in the Bible. My objective is to open not only my mind, but also the minds of others about the truths and possibilities of God's Word.

Since that is so important to my mission, God has opened the door for me to minister to young people and I have found that teenagers listen to me when I talk about these truths.

Once I made a visit to a maximum-security prison for violent offenders at Sand Springs, Oklahoma. There were 35 young prison inmates there. Most of them were murderers and rapists.

During the program I sang one verse of *Amazing Grace* in the Cherokee language and watched the face of an Indian boy glow. At the end of the program, those tough guys, really kids, gave the Lord a standing ovation.

Because of my love for youth, the Lord has led in the development of "Positive Attitude Assemblies" and has opened many doors for me to speak in school assemblies throughout the United States.

I am able to urge the students to apply the principles of success to their lives, to refrain from taking drugs, and to challenge them to be the best they can be. I want to help them understand that what lies behind them, what lies ahead of them, and what circumstances surround them is not nearly as important as what lies within them.

Yes, when I look at my accident, I know it was a tragedy. But I also know people who have suffered greater tragedies and have gone on to lead full and effective lives.

I want teenagers to know that in spite of what the world throws at you, even if it's a broken neck, it does not mean defeat if you really believe and apply God's principles to your life.

Before my accident, I had great plans to have a career in athletics. That changed. I could be depressed, blame God, and become bitter. That was not an option for me.

Even though most of the goals I set for myself the first year were pretty basic and selfish, they were goals - important to me in my determination to make the most of my situation and to become all that I could be.

Although it was about a year and a half before I knew the full direction of my life, I was determined to stay focused and make the best of my situation.

Today, God has given me direction - a better direction than the one I had chosen for myself!

Those same truths and principles are still in operation in my life!

"There is no failure except in no longer trying."
-*Elbert Hubbard*

CHAPTER SIX

When we played baseball at Tahlequah, we traveled in what we lovingly referred to as the "Green Weenie", a 1966 Pontiac Bonneville 8 door station wagon. In the far back, it had two small seats that faced each other toward the center of the vehicle instead of the front and would fold down to create a small cargo area, if needed. Because the cargo area was too small to hold all of our team's equipment, we had to use the whole next bench seat and floor for the equipment. So, a friend named Bill Hutson and I would flip up the back seats behind the equipment from everyone else in the car, play our guitars, sing our songs, and generally have the whole ride to ourselves.

One very hot spring day, we were going to Fayetteville, to play the University of Arkansas. Bill and I were sitting in the back seats, as usual, but the air conditioner was out of the Weenie, so we had them roll the electric rear window down so we could get some fresh air. We hadn't gotten out of Cherokee County when Bill and I realized that, if we didn't do something soon, he and I were going to be asphyxiated by the fumes that came from only 6 of 8 cylinders firing. Of course, the Weenie couldn't carry all 22 of us, so there were always a couple of guys who drove their own vehicles to the games. Bill and I waited until the next town of Westville,

Oklahoma, where we had to stop at the only traffic control device in the town, a four-way stop on Main Street. Without letting anyone else in the Weenie know, we quietly laid our guitars down in the seats, crawled out the back window, and got in one of the cars of our teammates following the Weenie. Shows you how much the team thought of us; they never knew we weren't in the Weenie until we got to Fayetteville.

Another time we had been to the right honorable Enos Seymour's home stadium at the University of Oklahoma in Norman. We got smashed on the baseball field, but we got to eat at their athletic dorm and cafeteria. We finished the best meal we had all season, climbed back into the Weenie, and the coach started her up. He couldn't see out the back window with all the heads and equipment blocking his view, so he yelled back, "Hey, Hutson, tell me how far back to come."

Bill hung his arm out the rear window and, as the Weenie began to roll backwards, he began to yell, "Come on back ... come on back ... come on back..."

I thought it was kind of strange, but after the Weenie had come several feet back and Coach had begun to back out of the parking space, Bill raised his hand high behind the tailgate. Trying to create a sound that would simulate a small crash, he brought his arm and hand down very flat, and with as much force as he could without hurting his hand. "Come on back ... come on back ...come on back ... POW! That's good!"

I began junior college as a music major at N.E.O. A & M College in Miami, Oklahoma, 65 miles from Salina. My ability to read music was extremely limited, but I always loved it, and I thought that's where I'd like to be. I was very ill prepared to be majoring in music, but I was doing as well as most, although I never had the focused goals in music that I had in athletics.

As a child, I visited Paw Paw and Maw Maw Collins. They had a radio that seemed to stand about nine feet tall. It had a record player that rolled out of a drawer in the lower part of the cabinet. They had some old 78-rpm records of the Chuckwagon Gang, a family gospel quartet from Texas. (I still love to listen to them.) I remember being able to hear and reproduce the harmony parts of those old songs. As soon as my family noticed me making up harmonies to songs on the radio, they had me singing all over our small town of Salina. I was about 14 or 15 before I began to realize that I had musical gifts that some other folks didn't have. Because our school was small - only 42 kids in my graduating class - we didn't have a real music program, but I sang in every Christmas program, at most of the banquets, and at two-thirds of the weddings that went on in Salina.

I played guitar for nine years before my accident and had developed a high enough degree of proficiency that I thought I might get lucky enough to have a career. I also had a couple of years of piano and some informal voice training, but in the years before the accident, I never considered that my talent for music was His gift to me.

It took time for me to realize this and how good God was to allow me to keep my vocal abilities.

CHAPTER SEVEN

Mom began taking me to church when I was in grade school. I had also been to a couple or three Vacation Bible Schools at the Methodist and Baptist churches in Salina.

When I was about five, we went to the Methodist church since we lived next door to it. When I was seven or eight we began going to First Baptist Church.

One Sunday morning when I was nine, God, the Holy Spirit, spoke to my heart to make me know how unclean we all are in our sin, how personally unclean I was inside, and that Christ could cleanse me and save me forever.

To me, accepting Christ, inviting Him into my life, was simply the best and sensible thing to do, so I did it! (Thank God for child-like thinking, for child-like faith! No matter how old we become, that's how we must come to Christ.)

I remember very vividly knowing the absolute cleansing of my total being by the Holy Spirit. I remember that, because God helped me to begin to understand the sacrifice Jesus had made for me, my total thought and action process was consumed by what would please God.

When I had thoughts that I knew were wrong, I said to myself, "I must stop thinking these thoughts." Or, if I was doing something that was not right, I told myself, "I must stop doing this, because God has saved me forever, and I owe everything to Him."

My brother, sister, and I played sports all of our school careers. Dad had been a coach for many years, so he and Mom helped and supported us as much as they could. We learned from Dad, along with our other coaches, the extreme significance of sacrificing time to practice and condition our bodies in order to prepare ourselves for a game. This included mental and spiritual conditioning and preparation.

Although my coaches were talking about the *spirit of the game*, after my accident, God used them to help me understand the scriptural principals of God that were involved which always apply to every part of our lives.

For example, the principle of self-discipline is straight from the word of God and applies from athletics to academics, from finances to personal relationships. This law cannot be altered. It is as true and everlasting as its Creator is.

We can be rich in finances, popularity, power, resources, recreation, pleasure, whether we are in Bangkok, Moscow, Tokyo, London, Rio de Janeiro, or in Mayes County, Oklahoma by applying certain exact universal principles. *I am not suggesting that we can simply name it and claim it.* I am saying that the principles of God are undeniably accurate and applicable without respect to person.

Remember my story about the "missed ball?" It didn't really matter what else I did or didn't do in my swing, if I missed the ball, the rest of my efforts were in vain.

When we begin to examine eternal things, it really doesn't matter if we learn and apply every other principle in the Word of God and have riches of every kind above everyone else in the world. If we miss the principle of eternal life through Christ, everything else is in vain. Christ said it best:

"For what shall it profit a man, if he shall gain the whole world and lose his own soul? Or what shall a man give in exchange for his soul? Whosoever, therefore, shall be ashamed of me and of my words... of him shall the Son of man be ashamed, when he cometh in the glory of his Father, with the holy angels" (Luke 8:36, 37, 38).

God helped me to understand that prayer is one of His principles. It is not just bowing our heads, closing our eyes, making some request, or saying thanks. Prayer is quiet, concentrated meditation on the Word of God, or communication to our hearts and minds by the Holy Spirit. That's why Christ told us to go into the closet (quiet place) and pray to the Father in secret. The Holy Spirit is born into our hearts, our subconscious mind. That's where He communicates to us and we to Him. He hears us and speaks to us in secret—one on one— personal (*Neat, ain't it?*). We can receive un-muddled communication. He can give us assurance, boldness, and ambition to do as He leads.

I have often wondered why I could go into the drawing board with the coach, be quiet, be taught, and be motivated to be obedient in what was required of me as an athlete, but could not, would not, believe that God, Almighty GOD, was worth listening to and being obedient to. I thank God for the lessons that He was able to pound into the natural reflexes of my personality, even though I was so resistant to coming to His house, learning from His Word and people, and was absolutely oblivious to my need to give Him praise, honor, and glory for His provision in my life through those principles.

God used those athletic endeavors to teach me the great physical rewards of setting aside some of those recreational things I wanted to do in order to accomplish those conditioning and skills-building tasks the coaches instructed me in - in other words, self-discipline.

He taught me unselfishness in considering, first and foremost, what would be beneficial to the team, instead of building my own career. He taught me that my needs and benefit were most completely served when I was intensely focused on how I could contribute to the team. (I'm still learning this one concerning the body of Christ.)

Along those same veins of unselfishness, He taught me that the *Spirit of the team* played a very important role in our success as a team. He taught me that I should be building my teammates up at every moment to make that spirit strong. I yearn, I long in my heart, to see the same team serving, up-lifting, building, and encouraging team spirit in our churches. Oh, how God can accomplish His work in us when we allow Him to develop that selfless attitude!

I was able to respond early to the absolute authority of the coach. God showed me later that all winning teams, from little league baseball to the 1991 war in the Persian Gulf, acknowledge the absolute authority of the coach, whether they agree with his decisions or not.

I was on many teams that were submissive to the absolute authority of the coach, but the coach did not have the specific ability in one or more areas to lead the team to championship. The Iraqis certainly experienced this dilemma in the above-mentioned war! Isn't it thrilling to know that our leader, our coach, is perfect, almighty, inerrant, eternal God who cannot lead us wrong, and that He's leading us through the victories in this world to the eternal reward He created for all who would receive His Son.

I once saw a beautiful creative road sign, which said, "HEAVEN - DON'T MISS IT FOR THE WORLD!" I agree with the message of that sign. There is nothing in this world worth missing Heaven for!

It is reassuring to know that the God of authority is busy working out all things for my good- for the good of all who belong to Him!

CHAPTER EIGHT

Sandi and I were already out of the van when Larry and Ann Floyd, our dear friends in Jacksonville, Florida, came bounding toward us, their faces plastered with those great big smiles that people wear when they are genuinely glad to see you. Our faces were no different.

"Hey, YoYo," Ann greeted me with a great big hug. Then stepping back, she asked, "How in the world are you?"

"As good as grape juice," I grinned, then added. "Thanks to the Lord and Sandi!"

When we were in school, Sandi was a few years older than I was, so we naturally had different interests and friends. We were not a part of each other's life. We knew each other in a friendly hometown sort of way, as we did everyone else in the twelve-grade, 600-student school, and 1,400 resident community.

Sandi began to come to see me regularly while I was in the hospital and rehab center. I was very grateful to her and the others who gave me and my mom and dad encouragement and assistance.

Sandi helped with all kinds of therapy. She brought books and read them to me. She began to learn to do the nursing/personal care duties that my mom would do when I got back home.

I wondered why Sandi insisted on learning those skills, but as time went on, I realized that she wanted to be able to give my folks an occasional break from that mammoth daily task.

I began to have weekend passes to go home Friday evening through Sunday evening. A week or so before Halloween, I came in from the weekend at home. Sandi, who was teaching first grade at Locust Grove, Oklahoma, was used to decorating for every occasion. She had decorated my whole room with Halloween's festive array.

This was the first time I saw the giving side of Sandi. Her pure giving spirit shows up in personal and loving gestures. Sandi is always making things for friends and family. I know that with every stitch or stroke of the brush or sandpaper, or nail, or screw, or bead of glue, that her heart is trained on communicating her fondness for the person she's making the item for. That's just the way she is! Always faithfully thinking about ways to show appreciation to those she feels have helped us.

As Sandi took on more and more of the duties involved in my care, we grew comfortable in the relationship that developed. After a couple of years, with neither of us planning it, our cordial, casual relationship grew to be a very real love.

I was very humbled that she could love me then. I'm daily astounded that she can still love me, with all the things she endures concerning me.

I love her, more today than the day we were married, more than ever before, and my love for her is growing more and more very day. I know I am a very fortunate man to have Sandi as my wife, and

I'm grateful to God for allowing me the gift of such a helpful, hard-working wife that loves me, and cares for me so well. I love you, Sandi, and I'm so very sorry for the burden I am to you, and thankful for your selflessness. I don't deserve your goodness to me, and I am forever indebted to you.

Proverbs 18:22 says, "He who finds a wife finds what is good and receives favor from the Lord."

On July 2, 1980, I gave Sandi her engagement ring. This is our engagement-announcement picture.

I know that the Lord cares about everything in the lives of His children, and nothing is too small or too unimportant that He is not interested. At every need, at every point, God has provided for YoYo and Sandi Collins, and I thank him for His provision.

After nine years as a teacher, I resigned for full-time ministry with YoYo, thrilled to be able to devote all of me to the ministry. My greatest desire in life is to be found faithful in what God has called me to do. I long to hear him say, *"Well done, thou good and faithful servant. Enter ye now into the joy of the Lord."*

CHAPTER NINE

YoYo Collins was the answer to my prayers!

It was 1980 and I had just returned from a date, a disgusting one. I was depressed and very low in spirits when I prayed this prayer from my heart.

"Oh God, I'm tired of trying to run my life and making a mess of it. Please, Lord, take over, and surely, God, there is a man somewhere that I could love more than any other person in the world. A man that I would love so much that I would put him first, would defend, be a helpmeet to, and most of all be a wife to."

I had married at seventeen, not knowing my mind. There was love at first, as much as I knew about love at such a young age. However, instead of growing together, we grew apart and our marriage failed. The two good things that came from the marriage were our precious children, Rhonda and Rodney.

After I was single again, YoYo Collins was among the men I was dating. We enjoyed being together. Shortly after his accident, I had assisted with YoYo on some of his rehabilitation exercises and tried to encourage him to find a life for himself. I thought his positive attitude toward everything and everybody was captivating. Then one day it dawned on me that I had fallen in love with YoYo. His kisses turned my heart over. This acknowledgement frightened me because I didn't know if he loved me. I also knew how much time was involved in taking care of him.

Then YoYo called me and said he needed to talk to me and the following evening I rushed home from the school where I was teaching first grade, cooked the evening meal, sent my children to a friend's house, and went to pick up YoYo, because at the time he didn't have a van that he could drive.

After dinner, YoYo said, "Sandra, I've grown to love you very much, and I would like to ask you to be my wife."

His words made my heart swell, but at the same time I thought about what a big commitment this would be. I had failed in one marriage and I didn't want to fail in another. I had already learned that life is not a fairy tale in which people simply get married and live happily ever after. I knew both partners have to work at it every day to make a good marriage, to keep the love strong.

I looked at him and said, "YoYo, I love you, too. I love you more than life itself, but please give me some time. I need to pray about it."

He agreed and through prayer came the strong assurance that with God's help we could handle anything that this world would hand us. When I told YoYo that I would marry him, he hugged me like I had never been hugged before.

The next day at school one of my friends shook her head and said, "You need your head examined. You will just be a nurse maid."

I protested, "No, I won't. YoYo is great. I love him and I believe that he loves me and, with God's help, we will have a wonderful marriage that will last the remainder of our lives."

My friend shook her head again and walked away, unconvinced by my optimistic enthusiasm and confidence.

YoYo had been singing since he was a small child and this was the talent that remained with him after the diving accident that paralyzed him. By the time he proposed marriage he already knew God was calling him to use this talent, but he didn't know where to begin.

"YoYo," I encouraged. "Give your talent to the Lord and use it to glorify Him." Then I added, "God has given me a talent for selling anything that I believe in. I believe in you. With God's help and direction, I believe I can sell your ability to serve Jesus Christ through your singing."

We meditated and prayed and then I picked up the phone. I called several pastors in our own association and scheduled YoYo to sing and share his testimony in several churches. On Sunday mornings I picked him up, we went to the scheduled church, YoYo sang and gave his testimony, and on Sunday evening I took him home. That's how we began.

On July 2, 1980, YoYo gave me my engagement ring and we set the wedding date for December.

Shortly after this, we attended the largest youth camp in the world, Falls Creek Baptist Assembly. On Tuesday morning, YoYo auditioned to sing in one of the services. Although he wasn't chosen, the woman in charge of the Oklahoma Baptist University Talent Show heard him and asked him to do the last twenty minutes of the talent show, giving YoYo the opportunity to sing to his largest audience up to that time. Several pastors heard him and invited him to sing and testify at their churches.

When school started, I put on the numerous hats I wore - mother, fiancé, homemaker, teacher, chauffeur, and a partner in ministry. To add to the hectic schedule, YoYo moved our wedding date up to October 14, adding loads of things to do to my already full schedule.

Our wedding plans included our pastor, Rev. Marion Dunham, my children who would light the candles and give me away, my best friend, Ramona Sheffield, who shared my happiness, as matron-of-honor, YoYo's brother Bennie, best man, his niece Heather Teague and Ramona's son, James, as flower girl and ring bearer.

Ann Fleming, Cecelia Speaks, Edna Earl Rice, and Joan Backward would handle the reception and Barbara Dodson and her daughter, Terry, would be in charge of the guest book and rice bags.

Barbara helped me decorate the church on Monday and Ramona helped on Tuesday. On October 14, 1980, at seven o'clock in the evening, YoYo and I were married.

Oh, how I cherished every moment of the wedding. The children lit the candles and my sister, Marsha Whalen, sang "You Light Up My life." When the wedding march began, YoYo, his brother, and Rev. Dunham entered. Ramona, looking beautiful in her long red dress, went down the aisle, followed by the flower girl and ring bearer. Then Rhonda and Rodney walked down the aisle and I knew it was my turn.

Extremely excited, I was so thankful to God for the moments I was about to experience. I felt the eyes of the guests on me and the next moment my eyes met YoYo's and stayed there.

The pastor asked, "Who gives this woman to be wed to this man?" Rhonda and Rodney said in unison, "We do." Then they stepped back.

From that moment on I was not aware of anything or anybody except YoYo, our pastor, Bennie, Ramona, and myself. After the pastor had us repeat the vows, YoYo was handed a microphone. He sang "Annie's Song" to me while tears of thankfulness filled my eyes.

It took a little more time than usual for us to exchange rings because YoYo was determined that he was going to place the ring on my finger. Then, the pastor prayed, pronounced us husband and wife, and introduced us to the guests as, "Mr. and Mrs. YoYo Collins!"

I clung to this moment that I had waited for so long. We exited to the tune of "Evergreen" played from a cassette, which YoYo had chosen to sing. He had recorded himself singing the song, adding to the recording piano music and a mocking bird from the wild. Rhonda and Rodney told us that the guests were looking around for the bird. It was beautiful!

One of the guests grabbed YoYo and hugged him, and as soon as he got loose, he put the chair in high gear. I had to almost run to keep up. Had I not been wearing a long wedding dress, I would have hopped on the bars on the back of the chair, something I now do in big shopping malls, getting several smiles from the other shoppers.

At our reception, family and friends greeted us warmly, loads of wedding gifts covered a table, and several of my school children came. Among them was Clint Ingersol who had a gift of four coffee mugs. He said, "I hope you like them because my folks made me use my money to buy them. They cost $40.00."

I think he meant $4.00, but I promised him I would take good care of them. I have kept my word. I still have them.

We spent our honeymoon in the beautiful Ozark Mountains in Eureka Springs, Arkansas. We had made reservations months ahead for the penthouse at the historic Crescent Hotel, informing the people that YoYo would be in a wheel chair. However, when we arrived, we found that the penthouse was accessed by way of a narrow winding stairway.

So we spent the night in a small corner room which reminded us of Grandma's bedroom, but we were so thrilled to be together as husband and wife, that we could have spent the night in a pup tent and it still would have been wonderful.

The days went quickly by as we visited the gift shops, ate in the fine restaurants, and stored up beautiful lasting memories. With our hearts and lives united by the Lord, we had begun our marriage.

"Dreams are the touchstones of our character."
-Henry David Thoreau

Sandi's parents, Raymond and Annabelle Whalen. Sandi
was by her father's side when he died in 1991.

YoYo's parents, Darwin and Fay Collins. YoYo's dad gave
YoYo his nickname. YoYo's mother died in 2003.

Rodney and Rhonda Coger gave their mother away at the wedding.

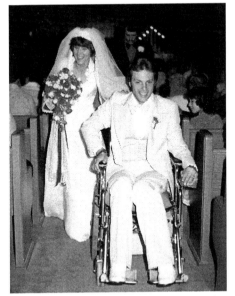

YoYo made a spirited exit down the aisle after the ceremony.

CHAPTER TEN

The days of being just us together ended and the reality of work and daily life set in. I disliked leaving YoYo alone during the day because I worried that he might get choked or that his catheter might clog. However, I knew I had to put YoYo in God's hands. If he needed my help, he could call the school and I could be home in five or six minutes.

In January, 1981, YoYo sang at the after-glow each night after the sessions at Oklahoma's Southern Baptist Evangelism Conference, which is a wonderful opportunity for the Singer Evangelists, because pastors hear them and often invite them to their churches. At this conference Clyde Cain, who was at that time the assistant Director of Evangelism for Oklahoma, invited YoYo to be on program at the Youth Evangelism Conference the following December. We were thankful to God for opening yet another door of opportunity.

YoYo's positive attitude and his love for all people seem to come natural for him. As does his faith. He quotes, believes, and lives by Romans 8:28.

YoYo is considered to be paralyzed from the neck down. Our doctor says it is a miracle every time he sings. God has spared him most of the problems quads are plagued with. In twenty-two years, he has had a few colds, fifteen or twenty urinary tract infections, one broken leg, two broken hips, and a tumor in his bladder. God has brought us through several challenges. YoYo has remained uncomplaining.

Our day begins with my getting dressed. Then I dress YoYo. I set him in his wheel chair and then we go to the sink to shampoo and dry his hair. Next YoYo shaves and brushes his teeth. All in all, the routine of getting YoYo and myself ready takes about two hours. Thankfully, Rhonda and Rodney were pretty much self-sufficient. Before we left for school, YoYo always had a devotion time with us.

Before long school was out and I was glad because by now we were singing and sharing almost every weekend.

That summer, we went back to Falls Creek Baptist Assembly, praying that YoYo would get to sing in one of the services this year. This time, praise God, he did! This exposure added many bookings to us. We did many cabin devotions. YoYo also did a concert in B.B. McKinney Chapel for anyone who wanted to come.

YoYo had cut his first album in May, 1980. It's title was *Shadrach*, which he remembered from his childhood, and many of his albums sold at the concert in the B.B. McKinney Chapel, where YoYo sang to a full auditorium. I marveled then, as I do now, of the wonderful talent the Lord has given YoYo. I am glad I encouraged him to use that talent for the Lord who gave it to him.

Although God gave me the best students I had in all nine years of teaching, life was extremely hectic for me when school started, leaving me no spare time between teaching and our growing ministry. Often we would get home around one or two o'clock on Monday morning and I would have to be at school, ready to go to work and face 25 first graders at eight o'clock.

I was grateful that I was able to plan special things for them and knew they could handle them. I enjoyed teaching and hadn't really wanted to lay the job down. I had paid a dear price to become a teacher. When I had been out of high school seven years, been married seven and one-half years, had two children, ages 4 and 1, I decided to go to college to become a schoolteacher. But at this time of my life I knew something had to give, as I couldn't keep up the pace forever.

Early fall we decided to cut another recording and try to get them in time for the Youth Evangelism Conference to be held at the Lloyd Noble Center in Norman, Oklahoma. Professional back-up singers and musicians from Christian World Recording Studios in Oklahoma City would do the back-ups. This meant YoYo had to spend quite a lot of time preparing for the recording, which we planned to call *Special Delivery*. It was the song he had sung at Falls Creek in the summer when the kids, all 5,000 of them, had given the Lord a standing ovation. Since that time the Lord has received many standing ovations, and that's exactly how we look at it.

Over the 1981 Thanksgiving holiday we got driving controls put in the van so YoYo could drive. In the fall semester Rhonda had taken driver's education and had passed her driving test on her birthday, January 8, 1982. When both Rhonda and YoYo were able to relieve me as driver, I found that my load was considerably lightened.

However, right after we put the driving controls in the van, we had been so busy that we had not had time to let YoYo learn to drive it. When school let out for the Christmas holidays, we went to my parents' farm. I set YoYo into the driver's seat, tied him in, and his first mile to drive again since his accident was done in a cow pasture. He laughed and jokingly said that he only killed two fence posts and one cow. I wish you could have seen the look of excitement on his face as he was gaining another freedom.

Although he had done great, he still needed more practice before hitting the open road, but he was soon ready and now drives almost everywhere we go. As of now, he has driven almost one million miles. While he drives, I am usually able to either read, rest, or catch up on some sleep. I am very appreciative of this!

With Christmas over, it was time to go to the Youth Evangelism Conference. YoYo had been talking to me about my resigning as teacher. God had also been dealing with me about it, but I was not ready to give it up. On the evening before the conference YoYo was booked to sing at First Southern Baptist Church in Del City, Oklahoma where Rev. Bailey Smith was pastor.

Bro. Baily's sermon about being totally committed to God's course and work was primarily for his congregation. They had outgrown the 5,000 seating capacity of their church and were going to vote that day about relocating. But the message really ministered to me and I thought that surely the God who made Heaven and earth could take care of and provide for YoYo and Sandi Collins and their children.

I went forward and prayed, telling God that I would gladly resign my teaching position in May, 1982. Almost immediately we were booked up for the next year.

The Youth Evangelism Conference was an exciting time. On Monday afternoon when YoYo began to sing, several people rushed down in front of the stage to take his picture. This startled him and he almost forgot the words to *Special Delivery.* Later, he said he remembered that I would be praying for him, and that helped him. When he finished singing, all 8,000 youth gave God another standing ovation.

Every time YoYo sang, my heart swelled with thankfulness to God for His beautiful gift that he gave to YoYo and for YoYo's willingness to use this talent for Him. We had been in the ministry one year and eight months and God had opened so many doors in that short time.

After Christmas break, I told my principal and friends that I was resigning my teaching position in May. They couldn't believe it because teaching positions were hard to find and they asked, "What if this? And what if that?" Some thought I needed my head examined. I was not worried. I knew God would provide for us.

I left behind the school, where I had taught for nine years, for full-time ministry. I had no regrets because I was thrilled to be able to devote myself totally to the ministry.

After I resigned, we were both thankful that I no longer had to leave YoYo alone during the day. The summer was spent doing God's work. We sang in churches every weekend and at several church camps. YoYo and I went to Falls Creek Baptist Assembly two weeks of the summer. He sang in a service each week. YoYo also was a personality at the Fellowship of Christian Athletes National Convention in July of this summer.

With my resignation from teaching, YoYo and I became a full-time team. We trusted God to give us opportunities for service and provide the means for our living. He has never failed us.

Whatever ye do, do it heartily as to the Lord, and not unto men.
Colossians 3:23

In 1999 we recorded our 14th album.

December is for family. Our grandchildren, Lonnie Dale Salyers, Brady James Salyers, Laura Ashleigh Coger, Jerrod Salyers, and (in front) Hunter Nicole Coger make Christmas even more special. Laura and Hunter will have a new little baby brother or sister in July! (This is being written in February of 2005). We'll have six this Christmas.

CHAPTER ELEVEN

When we first began the ministry, I called pastors and told them about YoYo. I asked them if they would allow him to sing and share in their churches.

The first time I called Bro. Johnny McCoy, at Gilcrease Hills Baptist Church in Tulsa, he was not in. I visited with his secretary who assured me she would tell the pastor about my call. In a day or two I called back, but again Bro. Johnny was not in. I finally reached him the third time I called, but he sounded less than thrilled when he said, "Okay, come on."

On the Sunday we went to Gilcrease Hills, YoYo sang and shared his testimony of how God was using him. He told how God had blessed him and touched his life. Bro. Johnny and the congregation seemed to enjoy the service because they invited us back again, and then again.

One evening we received a telephone call from Bro. Johnny saying that he and his family had been called to pastor the First Baptist Church of North Pole, Alaska. They would be leaving for Alaska really soon and would like to visit us one evening before they left.

February was our busiest month and we had no complete evenings available. However, we were singing at a local wedding one evening, so we invited them for that night. I prepared a meal and left it with Rhonda and Rodney to serve our guests while we were gone.

When we got home around 9 o'clock, we visited with Bro. Johnny and Patti. During our conversation, Bro. Johnny said, "YoYo and Sandi, I want to confess something to you. When Sandi called, I let you come because I felt sorry for you. But after I heard YoYo and was blessed so richly from his singing and sharing, I felt sorry for myself." He continued, "When you called my secretary the second time, I wanted to make sure that I wasn't there when you called back the third time, but I'm thankful that I was, because I would have missed one of the greatest blessings of my life."

Needless to say, that evening was a special one and we became closer friends. He told us before he left that he hoped to have us at his church in Alaska. We said that would be great and they left.

In a few weeks we received a letter from Bro. Johnny asking us to send him a date when we could come to Alaska, but we had no open dates in the year.

We were sharing at First Baptist Church, Carnegie, Oklahoma and went into a restaurant on Saturday evening. A couple sitting in the restaurant recognized us from a poster we had sent for promotional purposes and invited us to sit with them. We discovered they had worked in Alaska and we told them about our opportunity to go there, but that we were booked full. Sandra Lawrence said, "Cancel someone and go. You will love it."

We thought about this, and when we got home, I called a precious pastor friend, Ron Crews, in Madill, and told him of the opportunity to go to Alaska. He said, "Sandi, you reschedule us for a later date. You and YoYo go to Alaska."

When I called Bro. Johnny with the date, he told us to pray for the means for the financing for the trip. A few days later he called us and told about sharing the possibility of our coming with his people. That very morning on their way out from the church, one man handed Bro. Johnny a blank check and told him to go buy the tickets.

We made our first trip to Alaska in 1982, leaving Tulsa, Oklahoma on August 30, 1982, at 6:15 P.M., and arriving in Fairbanks, Alaska at 1:15 A.M., on the 31st. We had to change planes which was quite an ordeal, but the airline people were great. One of the many blessings to being in the kind of work that we are in is that God already has people ready to care for us on all trips.

When our plane landed in Alaska, Bro. Johnny came aboard to help us off. As we came around the corner of the gate, there stood a rather rugged looking man and a lady. It was Don and Toni Walker, the church custodian and secretary. They were both smiling and from that day they became great friends of ours.

The Tip Top Chevrolet dealer in Fairbanks had loaned Bro. Johnny a van that we could use and Don had built a board ramp. We had not been allowed to take the electric wheelchair on the plane because of the difficulties the batteries might have caused, so I thought I would have to push YoYo's wheelchair our entire time in Alaska, but I was wrong. Don pushed YoYo every step.

YoYo sang and shared in four services in the North Pole church. Then Bro. Johnny, Don, YoYo, and I made the ten-hour drive from Fairbanks to Anchorage for another service in Jewell Lake Baptist Church.

The drive was simply breath taking, almost dream-like, and everywhere you looked God had framed a beautiful picture. We saw the Alaska pipe line, a large glacier, and the red salmon swimming back up stream. I picked a beautiful bouquet of all colors of gorgeous wild poppies, Alaska's state flower.

Some of the people in the North Pole church arranged for a bush pilot, Colin Conkle, to fly YoYo and me to see the Alaska Mountain range. On the flight, we saw four of Alaska's big game: black bear, Dall sheep, caribou, and moose. I also saw two graceful swans swimming on a small mountain lake.

Colin had his fiancée, Patti, with him and they later came to church to hear YoYo sing. Patti and I became friends and correspondents.

While we were in Alaska, Don Walker dressed YoYo in a leather jacket, helmet, and goggles, and strapped him with a leather belt to the sissy bar of a ten-foot, nine-inch long Harley Davidson motorcycle. He shot out of the bus-barn grinning from ear to ear! He said he liked feeling his sideburns blowing in the breeze!

We made a second trip to Alaska in 1984, taking with us our son, Rodney. On this trip, we drove from North Pole to Colin's parents' home not too far from Slana, Alaska. When we arrived there, Colin introduced us to his parents, Bud and Lenora, Conkle, whose home was Eagle Trail Lodge. Colin and Bud arranged to take us to Tanada Lake in remote wilderness Alaska, about a 45-minute flight southeast of Slana. The plane was a two-seat Piper Super-Club, and its top speed was about 70 miles per hour. Colin grabbed YoYo out of his regular wheelchair, walked out on the pontoon of that plane, and threw him up in the cab like a hunk of moose meat. Then they strapped YoYo's wheelchair to the struts of the plane, Bud climbed behind YoYo's seat into the back fuselage, and they took off. Colin flew Bud and YoYo in to Tanada Lake from the small lake there at Eagle Trail. Patti, Rodney, Patti's dog, and I drove in the car about 45 minutes to another small lake much closer to Tanada than Eagle Trail. Colin spent most of our precious fishing trip serving as taxi, getting everyone to and from Tanada. They helped us catch and prepare several arctic grayling there at Tanada for our evening meal back at Eagle Trail.

On Colin's last taxi-to-the-car to go home, YoYo and I were left alone on that spectacularly beautiful Tanada Lake in the absolute wilderness for about 40 minutes. There were no houses, no roads, no power lines, and no one else that could see or hear us. It was 42 degrees in the middle of July. We huddled beside a little fire built of tundra/sage brush, with no sign of civilization as far as we could see in any direction. Whatever the opposite of claustrophobia is, I HAD IT!! I was sure glad to hear Colin coming back over that mountain in that little plane to take us back to the lodge. For YoYo, Alaska was a dream come true. He kept his nose pressed to the window of the plane, not wanting to miss anything.

In all, we have made 5 trips to the interior of Alaska, flying there on the last day of August, 1982, and staying during the first ten days of September, and in the mid-summers of '84, '85, and '87. In 1989 we drove the Alcan Highway. On this wonderful trip, YoYo drove all the way to Alaska and back. In 1993, we made our sixth trip, driving to the ferry to go to the southern-most Southeast Alaskan island city of Ketchikan.

During these trips, which were all a gift from God, we made many precious friends while doing the Lord's work. We have many souvenirs, (most of which were given to us; some of which I purchased), to remind us of these special times spent in Alaska. Altogether, we have made six trips to Alaska and we continue to thank the Lord daily for "The Experience of Alaska".

Oil and perfume make the heart glad; so a man's counsel is sweet to his friend.
Proverbs 27:9 (NAS)

CHAPTER TWELVE

1982 ended with YoYo singing and sharing in 220 different concerts. We feel humble and thankful that the Lord gave us this ministry. We also praise the Lord for His provision for us.

I'm reminded of a time when we were on our way back to the motel after a youth rally in Frederick, Oklahoma, when YoYo wanted a pizza. He was tired, so I went into the pizza place and ordered one to take to our motel. I went back to the van and sat with YoYo until I thought the pizza was done. As I approached the counter a man walked up and said, "Please, put her pizza on my ticket."

I said, "Who are you?"

He said, 'You don't know me, but I've heard of your and YoYo's work and I'd like to buy your pizza for you. But there's a favor I'd like to ask. Would you bring YoYo in and eat with us?"

This was the beginning of our friendship with Tom and Marsha Gaines. We have sung in their church many times. God is constantly giving us the friends, like Tom and Marsha, that we need to enrich our lives.

Once our van starter switch had been acting up, so on our way through Tulsa we stopped and bought a switch. We planned to have our friend in Salina, Oklahoma, who is a mechanic, fix it the following week. The van died as we were backing the trailer in to unload the sound system. The switch would not work at all.

A man was there to help unload the equipment and he had a friend with him who knew how to change the switch and had it fixed in ten minutes. He didn't just happen to be there. I believe God placed him there to help take care of a need we had, and I thank Him for it.

Several times people have called and needed to cancel or reschedule a concert and a few days later another opportunity arrived to fill the empty date. I know God is in control of our lives.

It is sometimes difficult for an evangelistic singer to make it financially because they usually sing in revivals and revival season essentially extends only between March and September. However, in our ministry, instead of our doing revivals, God has made it possible for YoYo to sing and share somewhere every Sunday, every month of the year, with the exception of December which we spend at home. This sometimes includes YoYo being a special guest during revivals on invitation of the pastor.

God does provide for our needs in many ways. For example, in May, 1982, YoYo's parents deeded us a 2 1/2-acre lakefront lot on which to build a home. We were planning to build a rather spacious single story home, but after hitting solid rock on a portion of the lot, our plans had to be changed. The new home would be a two-story one. We placed our old house up for sale, but it remained unsold as we built. We proceeded to build the new house as the Lord made the money available. Surprisingly enough, it came a long way in a year and two months. The outside of the home was completed and ready for the wood part to be painted. The inside was sheet-rocked and ready for wallpaper and paint. A portion of it had been paneled and textured. The kitchen cabinets were built and ready to be sanded, stained, and varnished.

Several friends donated labor on the house. Our friend Jerry Pritchett helped sub-contract out some of the work and he supervised the framing in and built the kitchen cabinets. He took no money for his labors.

Rev. Bill Nixon, who was then pastor of First Baptist Church, Blocker, Oklahoma, donated his labor for the wiring of the house.

Originally the house, a colonial style with large white pillars streaming down from the roof to the front porch, had 3,100 square feet of living space, but after two additions it grew to 5,500 square feet. It is dedicated to the Lord for his use and some day it may become a bed and breakfast or a retreat center, as He leads.

A desire of my heart since I was a small child was to live in a large two-story house on a lake. In God's word He promises to give us the desires of our heart if we seek Him and His righteousness first (Psalm 37:4). I look on this home as a true gift from God.

When it was completely finished the house was paid for and our old house sold. Once again, the Lord had met our need, this time for a home, in His perfect way.

One of YoYo's dreams since he was paralyzed was to have a van that allowed him to be completely independent. In 1982, such a van cost over $20,000. In August, 1982, a small church gave money to begin a van fund for him. The money wasn't much, but in less than a year others donated money and we had added a percent of the income from the ministry to the fund. The van was purchased and sat waiting at the handicapped equipping place in Edmond, Oklahoma until God provided the additional $5,000 to pay it off. Today the same van costs over $50,000.

The first money for the van was given by Hartshorne First Baptist Church. They sent their Vacation Bible School offering. Bethel Baptist Church in Owasso, Oklahoma gave a $1,000 donation. A group of youth from Freedom Hill Baptist Church, Mannford, Oklahoma held a rock-a-thon and raised $263. Several precious people gave gifts of five, ten, twenty, and one hundred dollars. One couple said that God impressed on their hearts to give $350 of their income tax return. An 83-year-old lady, who we had never met, heard of YoYo and the van and she sent $200. Brother Luther Williams, at Bartlesville, Oklahoma, who preached past retirement age and refused to stop working for the Lord until he went home to be the Lord, sent us his gas allowance check for one month to go toward the van.

YoYo and I do much of our traveling in a special van designed so he can do the driving. Although he is unable to use his hands, he has some use of his arms, which enables him to manipulate the special push-type controls. The steering wheel has small posts that he can slip his wrists between in order to steer.

YoYo has suffered (with a grin) two broken hips and a broken leg!

I can truthfully say that I enjoy this life the most when we are doing the concerts. I take care of the bookings, manage the ministry table, and run the sound equipment while YoYo shares and visits with the people, and run the sound equipment. The people are great at helping me bring in and set up our equipment. YoYo and I share the secretary work.

YoYo ministers to people of all ages. They all love him, but he feels a special calling to work with youth, and they do listen to him. He always has time for all people. He answers every letter he gets whether it's from a five-year-old or an 85-year-old.

We also believe that one of the most precious parts of our ministry is time spent with pastors and their wives. We love to fellowship with them, to listen to them if they want to share any problems or concerns with us, to pray with them, or just to be there for them in any way we can. Rich and lasting friendships have grown out of our spending time with these special servants of God.

If we have any private time we have to schedule it. I believe we appreciate our private time more this way. We are thankful for all God has done and is doing through us. I am constantly reminded that God can use us if we are willing to submit ourselves to Him and are willing to go wherever He sends us. Whatever He calls us to do, we want to be faithful.

And let us not be weary in well doing; for in due season we shall reap, if we faint not.
Galatians 6:9

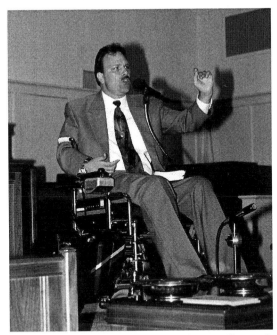

Often there is no easy access to the podium for YoYo, but, with the help YoYo's portable ramps, men in the churches roll him into position for sharing the gospel.

Great friends like Bob and Jo Mozingo are a gift from the Lord!

CHAPTER THIRTEEN

Sometimes people who are in love with someone who is paralyzed question me about the advisability of marriage. My answer is always the same. Marry only if it is God's will.

I knew I loved YoYo, but I needed the assurance from the Lord that I should marry him. I earnestly sought God's face in knowing whether or not we should marry. I did not agree to marriage until I knew that it was the Lord's will for me.

Marriages always have stress, but marriage to a quadriplegic is exceptionally challenging. It is very difficult physically because there are no days off. Even when I am ill, I still have to provide the physical care for YoYo—things like picking him up, bathing, dressing him, putting him to bed, and changing the urinary bags and the catheters. I never mind doing these things and plan to continue as long as I am physically able. Thankfully, God has given me generally good health and a strong back.

There are always adjustments in marriage. Our biggest adjustment centered around YoYo's parents who, because of their protective love, had a difficult time letting him go, a not uncommon problem for parents who see their offspring as a child and not as the adult he has become.

When we were first married, YoYo's dad, who has always been a wonderful man, helpful and kind to me, was so proud of YoYo's singing ability and had a great desire for YoYo to sing country music. On the other hand, YoYo and I believed that he should use his talent in serving the Lord. The tension grew and my constant prayer became, "Oh, God, please, fill our lives so full of you and your work we won't have time for other things." But, as family problems need to be resolved, we realized that we had to have a family conference. All the way to the home of YoYo's parents, I prayed about what I was going to say if the need arose.

During our discussion, his dad expressed his desire for YoYo to follow the dream that he had for him.

I listened to the discussion for a long time, but then I knew I had to ask, "Who gave YoYo his talent? Isn't that the one he should sing for?"

After that his parents began to let go. YoYo and I also knew that we needed to work on building a stronger family unit. We received counseling from a wonderful pastor who helped us to realize that while our parents were a part of our lives, our immediate family was our spouse and our children, and that should be our focus and responsibility.

All marriages are the same. They need work and care and ours was no different because of YoYo's paralysis. The paralysis affords a physical difficulty that other marriages might not have, but the major problems in our marriage were similar to every marriage. They were relational and this type of problem calls for a lot of give and take from every party involved in the relationship.

We are so appreciative toward YoYo's parents who have helped us, and continue to help us, in so many aspects of our lives. His dad was saved after our marriage and has become even more of an encourager to us than he was before his salvation.

Another problem that must be addressed when you are the caregiver of a quadriplegic is that of finding time for yourself, away from the one you are caring for.

We had been married for 16 years before I got that kind of time! YoYo, his dad, and his brother went off to Wyoming to hunt antelope for nine glorious days. I loved it! YoYo jokes that I missed him like a headache.

From my own experience, I would advise caregivers to take some private time. I find this time shopping with the girls. Often guys at a church where we are ministering will take YoYo fishing and I will go to the mall with friends. I have wonderful girlfriends in Florida and Alabama that I enjoy shopping with. It is a refreshing time.

Facing the truth of some very real facts is also important for the caregiver as well as for the quadriplegic. I have discovered that divorce is prevalent among this group and it is usually because 99% of the quadriplegics strike out at the caregiver who gives so much and often receives so little.

I am happy to say that YoYo has not lashed out at me and has a good, positive attitude. That has been a blessing in our marriage.

Joy has been present in our marriage. In 1983, during the months of May and September we were able to spend 2 1/2 weeks ministering in Hawaii - not a bad calling!

During that time we went to Disneyland in California and YoYo's cousin and our son Rodney lifted YoYo out of his wheelchair and placed him on many of the rides for his sheer enjoyment! And in

South Carolina two young men picked him up and took him out in a sailboat.

So we thank God for a full and blessed life, for each opportunity, blessing, and person He has placed in our path. The Lord has seen us through the good times, the trials, and tribulations. We praise Him for always being with us!

I will never leave you or forsake you.
Hebrews 13:5

CHAPTER FOURTEEN

The Lord has a way of opening doors. On New Year's eve, December 31, 1981, we were ministering in Stillwater, Oklahoma, first at a pancake breakfast for adults and immediately following that, at a lock-in for the teenagers of two churches. That is when God put Ron and Jayne White in our lives. Jayne was a professor at Oklahoma State University, in Stillwater, and Ron was a high school basketball coach.

"I broke my neck," Jayne told me, "But I only damaged nerves. I would like to visit with YoYo."

As it turned out, Jayne was doing her doctorate on quadriplegics and wanted to include YoYo in her study. After reading 15 different case studies she said that YoYo's case was very different. The comments placed in his records contained comments like, *"patient is too happy, has too positive of an outlook on life, hasn't accepted the reality of his paralysis yet."*

What the doctors didn't know, and I don't think YoYo realized at the time, was that YoYo, being by nature a positive person, had accepted his paralysis, but that God was also with him in a very special way.

Ron and Jayne went on interviews at Anderson College, Anderson, S.C. There they met John Edwards, a coach at the college, and his wife Phyllis, who told Jayne that she had a writer friend at Guidepost Magazine who would probably like to do a story about YoYo. Phyllis arranged for us to meet with Sue Monk Kidd, an outstanding writer, in Anderson, South Carolina.

Before we made the trip, I did what I call "cold turkey calling." I called Dr. Jim Crane, pastor at First Baptist Church, Anderson, and asked if we could share at his church while we were there. He was so kind and not only invited us to his church, he also scheduled meetings at Concord Baptist and at Longbranch Baptist.

Dr. Bob Marcaurelle, at Concord Baptist, put out the word that we would need someone to stay with. Lois and Gerald Riggins, who owned a dry cleaner in town, opened their home. Later Lois said the Lord "spoke to my heart but I was uneasy because I had never been around a quadriplegic."

After we stayed in her home she said, "After I was around YoYo for a little while I forgot he was in a wheelchair. He is such a joy and a blessing."

All of these people became our dear friends. Sue did write and publish her article in *Guidepost*, about four years later, in 1986. It was about how to grow hope and was well received.

The following year we were in Anderson, South Carolina and were invited to be guests on a two-hour interview and music show which ran from 10:00 P.M. until midnight on Channel 16 TV out of Greenville. We were interviewed and YoYo sang.

On the night of our interview a New Jersey pastor, Victor Coetzee, was vacationing in Myrtle Beach with his father-in-law and mother-in-law, and his father-in-law saw us on television.

The next morning the program was repeated at 8:00 and he told his son-in-law, "Victor, you have to see this young man. You have to have him in your church."

Later Victor Coetzee wrote a letter to us and I called him back. He is such a personable man. He said he would like to have us in his church, and would also like to schedule us in several other Assembly of God churches. I told him that would be fine and I scheduled four Southern Baptist Churches in that area also.

While we were in Franklin, New Jersey, we met a woman whose brother was a pastor in Alabama and when we got back to Oklahoma, Neal Chaffin called from Albertville, Alabama and said his sister had told him about us. He invited us to minister in his church. This introduced us to Alabama and since that time we have made so many friends in Alabama. Among them are Neal and Ameila Chaffin, James and Joyce Jolley, Sherrill and Patricia Jolley, Marvin and Joyce Beck, and Terry and Freda Duskin.

That is one of the wonderful ways the Lord has worked in extending our ministry—one friend seems to lead to another friend and ministering in one area seems to point to the next.

We have always gone to the Southern Baptist Convention since we became full-time evangelists. One year the convention was in Kansas City, Missouri and we put our brochures at the table provided by the Conference of Southern Baptist Evangelists. Many pastors come by that table and it is a joy to meet and talk with them. This year there was a cassette player and microphone and the singers took turns singing. Of course, YoYo was happy to take his turn.

It was in the early '80s when the feud between the liberals and the conservatives in the convention was raging.

Paul Callahan, who was then pastor at First Baptist Church, Warrensburg, Missouri, close to Kansas City, was at the convention and he tells this story every time we share in his church.

He said he was so sick of the in-house feud, so weary of all the confusion, that he left the meeting and walked down to the booth displays. When he got there he heard YoYo singing and felt the Spirit of the Lord reaching out to him through that voice. He followed the music and came upon YoYo sitting in his wheelchair singing and was uplifted. He always says, "That year I had to go to the basement to find the Lord."

At that convention, Gil Brink, who was on staff of the California State Convention, also heard YoYo and later called and wanted our material. He said he would very much like to see the California State Youth Evangelism Conference schedule YoYo.

We sent him our material and he scheduled us to be at Stein Road Baptist Church in Bakersfield, where Sid Peterson was the pastor.

While we were in the Fresno area where the state office is located we met many of the pastors. As a result we were in 15-20 churches in California that year and the next year they invited YoYo to come to the State Youth Evangelism Conference and then he was also on program at the State Evangelism Conference and returned again for a second Youth Evangelism Conference.

That is another way the Lord keeps us busy. When we are on program at a State Convention many doors are opened.

God not only has been gracious in providing us a full-schedule for service; he also meets our other needs.

Our ministry in South Carolina grew to the extent that we decided we needed to buy a small cabin to use as a base when we were there. Our budget for this was set at $25,000 because that was what we could afford to make payments on.

Two years before we had meet Martha Myers who had handed us her business card and told us, "I have a large home with extra bedrooms and even an apartment in the basement where you and YoYo can come and go as you please. You are welcome to stay with us any time. Just give us a call."

I remembered that card and I decided to call them. We ended up staying in Pendleton in the apartment of Charles and Martha Myers for six weeks, which was a great blessing. But an even greater blessing came out of it. We became the best of friends and in 1989 we traveled with them for five days, visiting, among other places, Mt. McKinley in Alaska. It was a precious time.

Any way, the first night we were there we were sitting around eating cake and drinking coffee and I said, "Do you have a newspaper?"

Martha brought it to me and I began to look through it and my eyes fell on an advertisement for an A-frame cabin for sale on Lake Succession, Iva, S.C—the price was $23,500! I immediately called the man to see if it was still for sale.

He said that it was, but that another couple was looking at it. When he found out that YoYo was in a wheelchair he was immediately discouraged and said, "You don't want it anyway. It has steps."

I hung up, also discouraged, and told YoYo what the man had said.

YoYo said, "Wait a minute, Sandi. Let's think this thing through. If the man hasn't had any experience with someone who is paralyzed he may not understand about making something accessible. We still ought to look at it. We might be able to build a ramp."

This made sense to me. I called the man back. He still didn't seem very interested in talking with me. He told me again about the couple that was interested in it, and that they were coming to look at it at 2:00 the next afternoon.

By now, I was determined to at least look at the cabin and I asked him, "Have they put any money down? Have they given you any earnest money?" When he told me they hadn't I said, "Well, then it's still for sale, isn't it."

"Yeah. I guess so," he agreed.

"Well, can we meet you there tomorrow at 1:30?"

He agreed and the next day we shared at a church close by. I was so excited I could hardly eat lunch. Three other couples showed up a few minutes after we got to the cabin and the man told them, "I'm going to show it to this couple first and then I'll show it to you, in the order that you drove up."

We saw immediately that it wouldn't be any trouble for a ramp to be added and I gave the man $500 earnest money, assuring him that it would not be any problem to work out the financing. I didn't know the Lord was already working it out for us.

That night we were to share in the church where Broadus Moody was pastor and we went to their home to spend the afternoon. When Broadus came in, we told him of our plans and he told us about Carl and Nancy Alley who he thought might be glad to lend us the money.

He called the Alleys and not only were they ready and willing to lend us the money, they also had a lawyer friend who would arrange for a title search and get the ball rolling. On Tuesday at 4:00, three short days after reading about it in the paper, we signed the documents for purchasing the cabin.

The Lord had put it all together!

We painted the cabin and spent one night there on a hide-a-bed. There was a trailer with a room attached next door and everyone told us we would love our neighbors. We didn't meet them until the day we left, however, but everyone was right. Al and Mary Southerland became very dear to us. Al volunteered immediately to mow our grass when we were away and we became like family.

The Lord continued to bless. Some men from Barker's Creek Baptist Church built a ramp; Charlie Myers, from Pendleton, who is in the asphalt business, made us an asphalt driveway; and Leonard Gallman, from Cowpens, South Carolina, built an additional ramp out of treated lumber to the top floor so that YoYo would have easy access to the bedrooms.

Later the Lord extended his provision in a unique way. Al and Mary moved their trailer and built a three-story home. They then became concerned that if we ever sold the cabin the new owners might not be of their choosing. They asked us to sell the cabin to them and continue to use it as though we owned it. For the first year we said no, but then we decided it was the best thing to do.

Good As Grape Juice

Tracing these relationships reminds me that our Christian relationships are eternal. Sometimes I yearn for one night at our home when all of our friends can gather at the same time. Then I remember that is what heaven will be - we will all be together forever!

When I begin to think of friends, the list is endless. In mentioning some I run the risk of leaving out so many. But one by one the Lord has put people in our lives.

Jack Rinks, pastor of Varennes Heights Baptist Church, in Anderson, kept telling us about his friend Wyman Copass who was a pastor in Kentucky and how he wanted us to go and share with him in his church. For two or three years we never had the time to call Wyman and schedule that area.

Then while at the Southern Baptist Convention one year, our pastor in Oklahoma, who also happened to know Wyman introduced us to him and we were able to go to his church in Louisville, Kentucky.

In 1998, YoYo was on program at the Kentucky State Pastors' Conference and more doors were opened for ministry.

We met Jim Butler, pastor of Cache Road Baptist Church, Lawton, Oklahoma, early in our ministry, at the Afterglow at the Oklahoma State Convention. We shared in his church. Later when he took the pastorate at First Baptist Church, Midwest City, a suburb of Oklahoma City, we went there. Next he moved to First Baptist Church in Lakewood, Washington and we traveled from California, where we had been sharing, to be with him in Oregon. Later he became the pastor of Calvary

-87-

Baptist Church, McAllen, Texas and we went there, too.

While there his wife LaWanda introduced us to a godly saint, Vivian Thompson, who was the kind of woman at whose feet I would love to have sat for many hours. We did stay in the guesthouse of this dear lady and one year on YoYo's birthday, January 11, she gave him a wonderful birthday party. She has since gone on to be with the Lord.

Each year in Mission, Texas, the Mayor's Prayer Breakfast and the High School Baccalaureate Service share a speaker. Vivian was one of the people trying to enlist someone for the program. That year they had hoped to invite Joni Erickson, but their budget prohibited it.

So Vivian asked if YoYo might like to come. We readily agreed. Mission is the place where a busload of teenagers who were returning from Youth Camp was swept away by the flood and eight or ten kids were killed. The terrible tragedy had brought the town back to God. The principal asked YoYo to share his Christian testimony. When YoYo finished, everyone was so moved that the Lord received a lengthy standing ovation and many hearts and lives were blessed.

While in Texas, we went on a mission trip to Old Mexico where I was overcome by the severe poverty of the people. It made me ashamed that I have so much and at the same time so appreciative of what God have given us.

When I was growing up we didn't have much, but it was nothing to compare with the absolute lack of basics these people live with. Many of them actually live in cardboard boxes.

We went strictly to minister and not expecting anything in return, but some of the churches wanted to take up a love offering for us. One church collected what amounted to $25.00 in U.S. money, a tremendous amount for such a poor country. We were so touched by their love and generosity.

I know thy works; behold I have set before thee an open door, and no man can shut it: for thou hast a little strength, and hast kept my word, and hast not denied my name.

Revelation 3:8

So far, our ministry has taken us from South Carolina on the Atlantic Coast to Hawaii (1984) in the middle of the Pacific Ocean.

CHAPTER FIFTEEN

Back in the 80's, we were talking about our wonderful trip to Alaska with a youth director in Western Oklahoma while sharing in his church.

He asked us, "How would you like to go to Hawaii?"

YoYo said with a big grin, "We ain't gone yet?"

He told us that while stationed in Honolulu when he was in the army, he became a friend of Pastor Ken Newman and his wife, Alice, who had treated him like a son. He said he knew they would want us to come and he gave us the Newmans' telephone number. Late one night when we arrived home after a four or five hour drive from the church where we had shared, I called Pastor Newman.

When I called, Ken said that he trusted the youth minister's judgment and wanted us to come, although his church would not be able to pay our way. He promised to get in touch with some other churches and see if they would like for us to share in their churches, too.

When I gave him a second call, he told me about two members of his church, Bob and Jo Mozingo, who were from Pryor, Oklahoma, which is our Mayes County seat. Bob, a few years older than us, had grown up in our town of Salina. Ken said they were so excited about our coming that they had convinced their church and five or six other churches to let us share.

So we were off to Hawaii. After a long flight, which began at 4:00 a.m. out of Tulsa, we arrived at the airport. Bob and Jo were there, smiling, with beautiful leis. Everywhere we went in Hawaii, people put these luscious flowers around our necks. When we went to hula shows, the girls always picked out YoYo to be the recipient of these flowers. YoYo learned to do the hula himself - with his mouth. Real cute!

Early in the ministry, while I was still teaching, a pastor of a small church in Oklahoma told me, "Sandi, if you ever need anything, tell someone. God uses people to supply the needs of his servants." I have found this to be true and have taken great solace and comfort from his words.

Being in Hawaii was like a honeymoon for us, but the personal blessings of Hawaii extended far beyond the two-and-one-half weeks we were there. Bob and Jo were real-estate agents. Less than a year later, they moved back to Pryor and opened an office. We became best friends, to this very day!

Another provision God gave us came out of our sharing at First Baptist Church, Waikiki. We were at the tape table and a man, most likely high on drugs, had come in off the streets and he wanted to talk with YoYo. While YoYo withdrew to talk with the man, JoAnn Thompson came by the table and introduced herself. Then she said, "We are from Bartlesville, Oklahoma. Jim and I are flying back home tomorrow for a couple of weeks because one of our sons is getting married. We have a two-bedroom condominium and a new car. You are welcome to both of them for the next two weeks."

What a blessing! We had planned to spend five nights in a motel and then the rest of the time in the home of a member of one of the churches. I had pushed YoYo's chair all the time we had been there—7 miles on the first day—and I was weary. How nice it would be to have a place like Jim and JoAnn's condo to relax in.

Once again, I was reminded that there is no need for us to worry when we go to a new area because we know that God already has people ready to take care of us. He has never failed us in all the years of ministry. He has provided our every need at every point. Our part is to *"seek ye first the kingdom of heaven, and all these things will be added unto you."* We are to put God first and *"He will give you the desires of thine heart."*

We, like everyone else, have experienced hurts and tragedies in our family and among our friends, but through it all God has been there.

Early in our ministry we sometimes had to leave our children with family members when we went on one of our tours.

I read a story about a missionary couple during World War II who had four small children. Where they lived there was constant bombing all around, so the parents decided to send the children to her parents where it would be safe. As it happened, the very place where they sent the children was the exact place where the next bombing took place. It was a long time before they learned whether or not their children were safe; it was so long that they had another child before they found out. During this time the Lord ministered to the mother's heart. He said to her, "Ma'am, you take care of what is entrusted to you and what is dear to me and I'll take care of what is dear to you."

The Lord spoke to me through that story and I can say with clarity that he has always been faithful to take care of us.

One special way God has made provision is in seeing that we were present at important times in the lives of our family. From the time our son had gangrene from appendicitis to the birth of all four of our grandchildren, everything we needed to be home for, we were. We schedule our meetings as much as two years in advance, so this is a real miracle.

Our granddaughter was supposed to be born on March second, while we were in Old Mexico, but she did not come until April 2, and we were there. It was a difficult birth. Robin had decided to use a doctor in Tulsa who her mother knew instead of one in Pryor. When we heard she was in Tulsa in labor we all fled to the hospital. Her labor progressed for seven hours and then she quit dilating.

Her doctor had dropped by and told her that he had plane tickets to Las Vegas and, if she had not delivered by 9:30, he would not be around for the delivery. When 9:30 came, Robin still had not delivered the baby and he did exactly what he said he was going to do. He left for Las Vegas!

Her contractions were hard and with each contraction the baby's blood pressure began to drop, but then it would come back up. Then suddenly it began to drop and did not rise. The attending nurse pressed the emergency button and called for the other nurses and doctors to get in there quickly.

I rushed down two corridors to tell YoYo, our daughter, and our son-in-law what was going on and then rushed back to find that they had taken her across the hall to the operating room. Three minutes later we had a baby girl.

I am convinced that had the baby been born in Pryor she would not have received the needed attention and would have died from the stress of birth, but the Lord protected her. And we were there! We were also present at the birth of each of three grandsons.

About seven years ago, at the age of 71, my Dad, a Christian who could not give up smoking and had emphysema, passed away, after having been sick for some time. I had always been Daddy's girl and I wanted to be home when he passed away. The Lord granted that desire of my heart and I was the one who held his hand when he drew his last breath. When the breath left my daddy's body, I felt like part of me died that night and my inner soul weighed a thousand pounds. God saw me through that time and today the bad hurt is gone, but the scars are there, and though God has given us a precious stepfather, I still love and miss my dad.

Our son Rodney was eight years old when he went forward at church and made a profession of faith, but there was never any fruit and I could only hope that he really had been saved.

When he grew up, he quit going to church. When I tried to talk to him about it, he said, "Mama, you made me go to church when I was at home. I'm not going any more."

It was very hard for me to accept that and I kept praying for him and trying to talk to him. Then the Lord spoke to me, "Just let him go." And I began to pray, "Lord, keep him safe until he gets right with you."

Ten years ago YoYo was the special guest at a revival, providing the music, and the preacher for the revival preached on burdens of our lost loved ones. He asked, "Are you willing for God to do whatever it takes for that person to be saved, even if it means losing your life?"

I had such a heavy burden for Rodney that I went down at the invitation and prayed for Rodney and told the Lord that I was willing for whatever it may take to happen for Rodney to be saved.

During the ten years that followed Rodney not only had gangrene, but he was also shot in the leg in a hunting accident. He and our son-in-law had been putting deer stands in trees. They both were wearing pistols. When they got to their pick-up, it had a flat tire on it, which they fixed. When Rodney put the car tool in the back of the truck it hit the hammer of the pistol and the bullet went into his leg and traveled through the muscles down the leg.

The doctor said to him, "Young man, I don't know if you believe in God or not, but you need to go to church Sunday and thank Him. Let me tell you what could have happened. The bullet could have hit the bone and shattered it. It could have hit a nerve and paralyzed your leg. It could have hit an artery and you would have bled to death."

But even through this experience, Rodney did not turn to the Lord. At my father's funeral in 1991, Robin was pregnant and she miscarried. Shortly after, Rodney's other grandfather died suddenly. On June 14, 1998, at the age of 54, Rodney's natural dad died suddenly of a heart attack. Through all of this, Rodney was not saved, although he did express concern about his father's salvation.

Before Christmas, 1998, Rodney's wife told him that she didn't love him any more and wanted a divorce. This crushed him.

December is the only time of the year when we are able to go to church with our family. I asked Rodney if he would go to church with us on Sunday morning, December 13, 1998. He said that he would. So Rodney, Robin, Laura, YoYo, and I all went to church at First Baptist Church, Salina.

A revival had just started with an evangelist named Ken Freeman. He was in his early forties and wore his hair cut short. In the back of his head a cross was shaved out of his hair. I was a little skeptical, but when he started preaching I knew the Lord had told him that people in Rodney's condition were present because his sermon was right on target. At the invitation, Robin went to the front to pray and YoYo leaned over and said, "Rodney, you need to go pray with her."

Rodney went down and prayed and after the service, I told him, "Son, we know about your problems and we want you to know we love you and we are here for you."

"Thank you, Mama," he said.

Wendell Lang, our pastor at First Baptist Church, Pryor, where we are Staff Evangelists, had a staff Christmas party that Sunday night that we attended. When we got home, the telephone rang. It was Rodney and I heard the most wonderful words I could hear. "Mama, I got saved tonight. I feel like I can fly. I feel like all the weight is gone."

I said, "It is, son. All your sins are gone now and forever."

I was so happy. It was the best imaginable Christmas.

I tell this story as an encouragement to parents of grown children who are not saved. Don't give up even if your words seem to fall on deaf ears, because there is still hope. I also think that often someone else can talk to our grown children when we can not. I might not have picked Ken Freeman to be the one to reach my son, but Ken Freeman is an anointed man of God. I am most thankful for all of God's messengers.

That if thou shalt confess with thy mouth the Lord Jesus, and believe in thine heart that God hath raised Him from the dead, thou shalt be saved. For with the heart man believeth unto righteousness, and with the mouth confession is made unto salvation.
Romans 10:9-10

CHAPTER SIXTEEN

Over the past eighteen years, as we have traveled about the country sharing and singing for the Lord, we have been the recipients of special blessings from the Lord who has met our needs in a variety of ways.

During the month of February, in the mid-80's we were staying in a motel while sharing at a church in Oklahoma City and I had just put YoYo to bed when the telephone rang at about 11:15. It was the man at the front desk and he wanted to know if we were the owners of a particular van. When I told him that we were, he said I needed to come downstairs because it had been burglarized and the police needed to talk with me.

The security guard had surprised the thieves, but they had gotten away, taking with them our microphones and tape players and my little short fake fur coat. I don't know why they took the coat because it certainly wasn't valuable, but it was something that I happened to like a lot. Because we are in and out of buildings so much, I don't often wear a winter coat, but this was one that had caught my eye and I enjoyed wearing it.

We knew we would have to replace the microphones and tape players right away, but I told YoYo, "When they put coats on sale in the Spring I'll buy another one." But time went by and I never did. I just managed to get by without one.

A year later we were sharing at a Youth Valentine's Banquet at First Baptist Church, Weatherford, Oklahoma. The pastor, Barry Camp, told us that his wife Martha would be with us for the first part of the banquet. However, she and some other women in the church had just finished the Christian Witness Training and they planned to go out that night and visit in some homes and witness.

Martha sat across the table from me. After we had chatted a few minutes she asked me if I would leave the room with her because she had something she wanted to ask me.

We went just outside the door and she said, "Sandi, are you allergic to animals?"

"What a strange question," I thought. Pastors' wives have asked me many questions, but this was a new one. However, I assured her that I wasn't allergic to fur.

She said, "The Lord told me to give my coat to you." And she took off her short rabbit coat and gave it to me.

I was so surprised and looked at her, puzzled. "Did you know my coat was stolen a year ago?"

"No," she replied. "But I know the Lord wanted me to give you my coat, and I want to be submissive to Him."

Later I told YoYo, "The Lord's probably going to give her a mink coat for giving me her rabbit coat!" I was laughing, but knowing how the Lord takes care of his children in even the smallest detail, I certainly knew it was possible!

Wayne and Betty Benson, dear friends, were assigned to the Pentagon right before Wayne retired from the military. He invited YoYo to share in a chapel service at the Pentagon, and we were thrilled to be able to tour this great building and to do a service there.

A couple of years later they invited us to come back to D.C. While we were there they had to go to South Carolina because Betty's niece was being pinned as an R.N. and they wanted to go to the service.

They turned their house over to us and told us to make ourselves at home and use anything in the kitchen we wanted.

On Friday it turned off chilly, so I decided to make some potato soup. When I looked in the kitchen there were no onions. Betty has a sensitive stomach and doesn't buy food that will upset it. So even though we really wanted potato soup we put it out of our minds.

That night YoYo starting feeling ill and Saturday morning we decided we had better run to Wal-Mart to get his prescription filled.

It wasn't easy finding a Wal-Mart in Washington D.C., but we finally did. I left YoYo in the van and ran in and got the prescription, then hurried back to the van.

Just as I was getting into the van, there on the pavement by my door lay a great big red onion. "Thank you, Jesus," I said, and holding it up, I told YoYo, "Potato soup."

I don't know how the onion got there; I don't care. The Lord put it there for our enjoyment. That's the way He provides for us! And because He even cares about providing the food we like to eat, I know that He will make provision to meet all our needs.

A couple of summers ago, I was putting on my make-up. I was talking to the Lord. I said,

'Lord, I'm just about out of this make-up. I need to find a Mary Kay dealer." Since we travel around so much I use one wherever I can find her. That morning the last person at our tape table was an attractive woman about 35 years old. I complimented the beautiful necklace she was wearing.

She said, "Thank you. I won this selling Mary Kay."

"Thank you, Jesus." I whispered because he had provided my need by sending me my salesperson.

I gave her my order and arranged for her to bring me my foundation at lunch. She did and I paid her for the merchandise. Between Christmas and New Year's a little brown box arrived in the mail. Inside was the beautiful necklace I had admired that morning, with a note from the Mary Kay lady. It said, "The Lord told me you would enjoy this a whole lot more than I would."

I wept and thanked Him again for his precious provision of a gift that I had neither asked for nor expected.

That same summer I wanted some cucumbers to make my lime water pickles that I make about every two years to put in chicken and tuna salads. YoYo's uncle had been giving us one or two cucumbers to eat, but you need quite a few for pickles.

We went to Haven Heights Baptist Church, in Fort Smith, Arkansas to share. We went to a nice couple's home for lunch. While I was helping the lady prepare lunch she said, "You wouldn't happen to need some cucumbers would you? I have a brown grocery sack full and you can have all of them if you want them."

"Thank you, Jesus," I prayed.

Another time we had been trying to find dead bolt covers to put on some cheap doors we had installed and we didn't want to buy double locks for them. We hadn't been able to find any. While sharing in churches in Tennessee, we went home with one of the couples in the church. He turned out to be a locksmith. You guessed it! He gave me the dead bolt covers.

"Thank you, Jesus!"

Over the years I had wanted some of the big beautiful hybrid Rose of Sharon bushes, but had never been able to get any.

Then we went to McMinnville, Tennessee. As we drove along I began to notice field after field of the bushes. I discovered that the area has the top nurseries in the United States for that type of bush.

Later I mentioned to the pastor how beautiful they were and how I had wanted some for such a long time.

He picked up the telephone and called one of his members who owned a nursery and that night they brought me three of those gorgeous Rose of Sharon bushes.

"Thank you, Jesus."

For a long time, I tried to find a ceramic kiln, but every time I saw one advertised for sale in the Sunday paper and called about it, it had already been sold. I grew discouraged about ever finding one.

YoYo said, "Don't be discouraged. God is just saving the best one for you."

Five years ago on Easter Sunday we were sharing in McAlester and I saw one listed in the Tulsa paper. The kiln was in Bartlesville and I called the number off and on throughout the afternoon, but there was no answer.

About 9:00 that night we started home and YoYo stopped the van and I called the number one more time.

This time the lady answered and I told her not to sell it, that I would come the next day and buy it. It was computer programmed with push buttons - just set them and it was ready to go. A perfect kiln!

"I told you," YoYo grinned. "God was saving the best for you!"

Another way the Lord has taken care of us is in the matter of personal safety while traveling so many miles in our van. Every time the van has broken down there has always been someone there able to fix it and get us on the road again.

For instance, we were driving in our van from South Texas to Denver in 1989, pulling a white utility trailer, when I was suddenly awakened from my sleep by a loud banging noise. I knew we had hit something. YoYo pulled over and I got out to check, only to discover that we had hit one of those plastic orange barrels the highway department sets up along the road during construction. Apparently the wind had caught one and had blown it out in front of the van. YoYo had run over it.

The barrel was hung up under the van and I had to grab it and hang on to it with all my strength while YoYo backed up.

With the release of the barrel, we went on in our van thinking everything was all right. Then we noticed in the right rear view mirror that one of the wheels on the trailer was wobbling. Again, YoYo stopped and I got out and discovered that the whole inside of the rim of one of the wheels was broken all around, although we had not hit the barrel with the trailer, but with the van.

But it just so happened that we were right upon the little town of Memphis, Texas. And it just so happened that there was a guy in this town who did nothing but fix flats. And it just so happened that there were still five minutes left before his closing time. And it just so happened that he had the needed rim and was able to change it. We paid our $20.00 charge and were on our way in a matter of minutes.

Now you and I know that *nothing* "just so happens" in the life of a Christian. God was taking care of us that time just as he takes care of us every time we get in that van!

More recently, we were traveling to western Oklahoma when we stopped and I ran into Wal-Mart to get some medicine for YoYo. When I got back to the van, YoYo grinned, "Sandi, while you were gone a hunger craving came on me."

We were on 69 Highway headed toward 412 to Tulsa, then through Oklahoma City to Chickasha, to share in two school assemblies. In Chouteau, south of Pryor, there is a Mennonite restaurant, which sells the best cashew brittle you have ever tasted. I knew that was where we were headed.

YoYo pulled off the road and into the parking lot of the restaurant. At that moment the control hook to the gas pedal and brake fell apart. We looked at each other and we both knew that, had YoYo not had that craving for cashew brittle, we would not have pulled off the road and we might have had a bad wreck in which someone could have been killed.

I was reminded again that there is an appointed time for each of us to die, and before that set date, God is going to do whatever is necessary to protect us.

In all of the years that we have been driving up and down the road, we have had only two real close calls, which could have been head-on collisions. Both were in Oklahoma, late at night, during severe rain, and the other driver was on the wrong side of the road. Both times at the last split second, YoYo whipped the van out of harm's way. Surely the Lord had his guardian angels there to protect us.

To a non-believer, some of this may seem either silly or inconsequential, or maybe even circumstantial, but not to me. I know that the Lord cares about everything in the lives of His children and nothing is too small or too unimportant that He is not interested. These stories are only a few of the many, many times that God has met our needs.

At every need, at every point, God has provided for YoYo and Sandi Collins and I thank Him for His provision.

But my God shall supply all your needs according to His riches in glory by Christ Jesus.
Philippians 4:19

YoYo was even upbeat when he reached the big 4-0, in 1994! Optimism has always been a part of his emotional make-up. His positive message of serving Jesus with all your heart is well received by young and old alike.

CHAPTER SEVENTEEN

God has blessed us in the all-important matter of health. I am rarely ever ill and I have been given the physical strength to care for YoYo. Also, for the most part, YoYo has probably been the healthiest quadriplegic we have ever known.

Once, from all the lifting and the pulling on of his clothes I have to do, along with the general difficulty and strenuous physical activity that is involved with taking care of a quadriplegic, I developed a painful tennis elbow. About that time, YoYo developed a pressure point sore, which put him down for three weeks, and my arm got better. I teased him, "The Lord gave you the sore so my tennis elbow could get well!"

Because he has stayed so physically fit, we were surprised when throughout most of 1997, YoYo began to experience abnormal spasms in his legs. At first we thought it was probably from an irritation in his bladder. We went to a specialist who did a bladder scope and discovered a tumor in YoYo's bladder. The doctor assured us that he did not believe it was malignant and that we could wait on surgery until we had finished our commitments, so he scheduled surgery for December 16, 1997.

This time, although it was outpatient surgery, the doctor put him under general anesthesia because during the earlier bladder scope YoYo's blood pressure increased to stroke level.

YoYo came through the surgery fine, but four days later, on Saturday, the area they had cauterized broke and he began to hemorrhage badly. We rushed him to the hospital where they checked him. They told us to bring him back the next morning. We discovered that he was losing about a pint of blood per day and that he would need to lose four pints before they could give him a blood transfusion. The reason they waited is because of the high risk of aids. When a person is exposed to the aids virus it does not show up until about a week to ten days later, so when people give blood they may get a negative aids virus reading, but later it may show up positive and the blood is contaminated. The person receiving it can get aids.

YoYo was so exhausted he could not sit up. When he tried, he passed out. I came downstairs and thought, "I am going to call some pastors and get them to start a prayer chain."

I called our pastor, Wendall Lang. I also called Bob Jolly, the pastor, and Anna Brennaman, the educational director, at First Baptist Church, Cummings, Georgia. I told them about YoYo's serious condition and how pale he was and asked them to start a prayer chain. They assured me they would.

Within five or ten minutes after I made the calls, it was as though a switch was flipped - it was that instant! I checked and the dark blood that YoYo had been losing had turned to pale yellow urine. I watched and there was never another drop of blood. It was very apparent that God had healed YoYo.

He regained his strength and we were able to go back to ministering! 1998 was the healthiest year YoYo has experienced since he has been paralyzed.

I don't know why God miraculously heals some and not others. I can't answer that question. But I am thankful that He healed YoYo. I am thankful that he has given us this ministry and given us the desire to do the ministry that He has called us to do.

My greatest desire in this life is to be found faithful in what God has called me to do. I long to hear Him say, "Well done, thou good and faithful servant. Enter ye now into the joy of the Lord."

When I look into the face of my husband, I am overcome by the thought of how tightly woven together our lives have become. The prayer that I offered back in 1980—that God would give me a man I could love more than any other person in the world, a man that I would love so much that I would put him first, would defend, would be a help meet to, and most of all be a wife to—has been answered.

Today, I am overcome by the strong realization that there is no Sandi without YoYo, no YoYo without Sandi, and no YoYo and Sandi without God!

I would not have it any other way! Thank you, Lord.

I can do all things through Christ who strengtheneth me.
Philippians 4:13

About YoYo and Sandi Collins

No book can tell the complete story of any individual. Likewise, *Good as Grape Juice* gives only an introduction to YoYo and Sandi Collins. YoYo's injury was in 1977; his first public appearance was April, 1980; and he and Sandi were married in October, 1980. They have been sharing ever since.

YoYo and Sandi have taken their message to more than two-thirds of the United States, including: Alabama, Alaska, Arizona, Arkansas, California, Colorado, Florida, Georgia, Hawaii, Illinois, Kansas, Kentucky, Louisiana, Maryland, Maine, Michigan, Mississippi, Missouri, Nebraska, New Jersey, New Mexico, New York, North Carolina, Ohio, Oklahoma, Oregon, South Carolina, South Dakota, Tennessee, Texas, Utah, Virginia Washington, and Wyoming. They have also served in Mexico.

Their story continues through the lives they have touched. In addition to churches and religious organizations, YoYo shares in Positive Attitude Assemblies and as Commencement Program speaker for public schools. He also speaks (and sings) before business and civic groups.

YoYo and Sandi were featured in the June, 1986, issue of *Guidepost* magazine, and have been guests on several television programs, including the Trinity Broadcast Network.

YoYo served as president of the Oklahoma Conference of Evangelists for two years and as vice president for two years. Sandi served as the organization's secretary/treasurer and as vice president for two years.

The fifth chapter of the Gospel of John tells about Jesus healing a lame man. While God in His sovereign grace does chose to heal, at other times God does not heal, but He uses trials to reveal His glory in other ways.

YoYo and Sandi continue to be an example of growing better—not bitter—through adversity.

Partial Listing of YoYo's Appearances

National Southern Baptist Convention, 1983-88, 1990
Oklahoma Baptist's State Pastors' Conference, 1982, 85, 88
Oklahoma State Evangelism Conference, 1982, 1995
Falls Creek Baptist Assembly, 1981-83, 85, 88
Alaska's State Pastors' Conference, 1986
Arizona State Pastors' Conference, 1990
Arkansas State Youth Evangelism Conference, 1984
California State Youth Evangelism Conference, 1989
Florida State Pastors' Conference, 1991
Georgia State Couples in Ministry Conference, 1989
South Carolina State Pastors' Conference, 1992-93
Mississippi State Pastors' Conference, 1992-93
National Convention, Fellowship of Christian Athletes, 1982
American Business Women's Regional Conventions:
      Oklahoma, 1985-95
      South Dakota, 1991
      Kansas City, 1986
Oklahoma State Rehabilitation Convention, 1986
Oklahoma County Elected Officials' Convention, 1992
Mayor's Prayer Breakfast, Mission, Texas, 1991
Baptist Hill Youth Camp, Mount Vernon, Missouri, as
      Camp Pastor, 1991
Oklahoma County Assessors' State Convention, 1992
Missouri State Pastors' Conference, 1993
Utah-Idaho Southern Baptist Convention, 1994
Utah-Idaho Pastors' Conference, 1994
Easter Seal Society's Northwest Regional Convention, 1994
Tinker Air Force Base Handicap Awareness Banquet, 1994
Southwestern Bell High Achievers' Retreat, 1995
Wichita, Kansas Quarter Horse Show, 1995
United States Pentagon, 1992
California State Pastors' Conference, 1996
National Conference for Church Leadership, Ridgecrest, 1996
Kentucky State Pastors' Conference, 1998
Chaplain of Oklahoma State Senate, 2005

Additional Information:

If you would like to order additional copies of *Good as Grape Juice*, send payment to:

YoYo Collins
PO Box 819
Salina, OK 74365

Copies are $16.95, plus $1.50 shipping and handling. Include your name and complete address with your payment.

Call for quantity prices.

For information on YoYo's recordings, write him at the above address or email him at:
yoyo@yoyocollins.com

Check his web site for additional information:
www.yoyocollins.com

or call (918) 434-5949

YoYo and Sandi are available for your church, business, or organization.

For scheduling details, call or email YoYo at the above address.